Learn to Relax

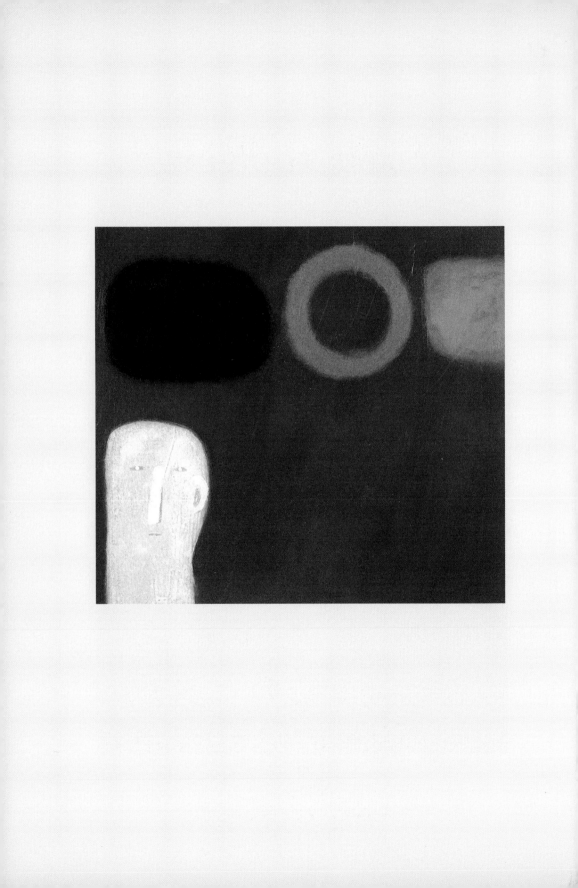

Learn to Relax

A PRACTICAL GUIDE
TO EASING TENSION
& CONQUERING STRESS

Mike George

CHRONICLE BOOKS

SAN FRANCISCO

Learn to Relax
Mike George

First published in the United States in 1998 by Chronicle Books.

Copyright © 1998 Duncan Baird Publishers
Text copyright © 1998 Duncan Baird Publishers
Commissioned artwork copyright © 1998 Duncan Baird Publishers
Sarah Ball's illustrations copyright © 1998 Duncan Baird Publishers,
except for those listed on p.159, which is to be regarded
as an extension of this copyright page.

Conceived, created, and designed by
Duncan Baird Publishers
Sixth floor
Castle House
75–76 Wells Street
London, W1P 3RE

Editorial consultant: Peggy Vance
Editor: Judy Dean
Designers: Jeniffer Harte, Richard Horsford
Commissioned artwork: Sarah Ball, Trina Dalziel

Library of Congress Cataloging-in-Publication data

George, Mike.
Learn to relax : a practical guide to easing tension and
conquering stress / by Mike George.
p.   cm.
Includes index.
ISBN 0-8118-1908-6 (pb). ISBN 0-8118-2104-8 (hc).
1. Relaxation. 2. Stress management. I. Title.
RA785.G46   1998
155.9'042--dc21   97-33259
                                                       CIP

Typeset in Mrs Eaves.
Colour reproduction by Colourscan, Singapore.
Printed in Singapore.

Distributed in Canada by
Raincoast Books
8680 Cambie Street
Vancouver, B.C. V6P 6M9

1 3 5 7 9 10 8 6 4 2

Chronicle Books
85 Second Street
San Francisco, CA 94105

Web Site: www.chronbooks.com

Dedication

With love to the One
who is eternally relaxed,
and to my spiritual family,
for whom "chilling out"
is a way of life.

Contents

Introduction

Ours is a world of explosive change, the breeding ground for uncertainty, insecurity and anxiety. While some believe that stress is necessary to reach peak performance, there are many more for whom stress is the cause of debilitating illness.

If we look back only a hundred years, a heart attack (one of the more serious stress-related diseases) was a medical curiosity. Might this be because it was much easier to relax a century ago? This was a time when the quality of being was more important than the quantity of doing — when people themselves were human beings rather than human "doings".

Although we can't go backward in time, we can learn to re-construct a much healthier and more relaxed lifestyle for ourselves, and to find again some of that lost peace. The only condition is that we have to want to.

In the early 1980s, I found myself suffering from enormous amounts of stress. At the time, I did not call it stress, I simply called it pain. I was working long hours, seven days a week, driven by deadline after deadline. My relationships were far from harmonious, and the one that suffered above all was my relationship with myself. Taking some months to research my pain, both internally and externally, I tried to find solutions. I knew that I had to change my lifestyle, and that I had to learn new skills, such as creative visualization and meditation. My research was thorough and intense, and it resulted in my discovery of the root causes of human distress at various intellectual, emotional and spiritual levels.

Thankfully, I discovered that the greatest gift I could give myself was the ability to re-connect with the state of peacefulness that had been present all along at the heart of my own being. I realized that it was possible to form and sustain loving

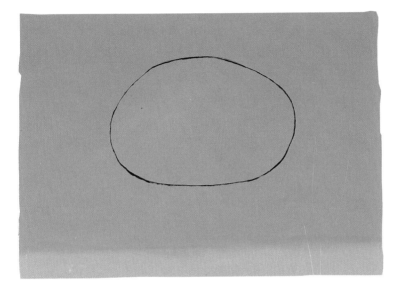

and harmonious relationships with others only when I was able to accept and love myself. And I found that no book, seminar or guru could do this work for me — although they often served to remind me of the next step in my journey through darkness and illusion. As light dawned, change became possible through the power of personal action and restored spirit.

This book serves as an anthology of some of my learning. Its aim is to pass on to you a selection of the most valuable insights that I have gleaned in my years of self-discovery. Through its thoughts and exercises, I hope that it will encourage and guide you, so that you too may understand and be reminded of the deep wisdom of relaxation. This wisdom lies not out of reach, in a far away place, but hoarded within each of us, simply waiting to be re-discovered.

Mike George

Roads to Relaxation

We all have a choice. We can live life in the "fast lane", pushing ourselves hard from one experience to the next, until one day we can push ourselves no more; or we can turn off the superhighway to follow quieter, slower roads that encourage our driving skills, rather than our driving speed. Ultimately, we may reach the same destination. However, the different routes by which we travel there will determine the state of our mind and body on arrival.

Perhaps we have forgotten how to make such choices. Certainly, for many of us, the fastest route seems the obvious one. Yet we sacrifice so much in taking it. We miss the fascinating views of landmarks and scenery, as well as the sheer charm of following a quieter road. The routes to relaxation are winding, with many turnings. We may even lose our way from time to time, but that all adds to the fascination, the sense of adventure and surprise.

Leaving the superhighway can prove difficult. Even if we resolve to try one of the roads branching off to left or right, unless we dispel the deep-rooted thinking that made us want to take the fast lane in the first place, we shall soon find ourselves back there.

Relaxation cannot be hurried. We must have faith that our slow, circuitous journey will take us in the end to the land of calm perspectives — the place we all dream of in our hearts.

World, Mind and Body

Some modern thinkers subscribe to the view that everything in the universe is connected by invisible threads of causality. Our mind is connected to our body, and our body to everything around us, from the vibrations of our footsteps as they pass into the earth to the sound waves that travel through the air each time we speak. This idea expands right out to the very edges of our world and, beyond that, to the heavens.

We have all heard the adage that if a butterfly flaps its wings in Japan, there is a hurricane in New York. Everything is energized, and we cannot be insignificant because energy is never lost. Each expenditure of our energy has incalculable repercussions all around us. With this in mind, we can challenge the state of so-called "esoteric" stress, the deep unrelaxation triggered when we sense our meaninglessness in the universe.

Despite this far-reaching web of connections, many of us withdraw into our individual caves and set imaginary limits to the sense that we have of our own potential. We might begin to doubt, for example, the value of our own opinions. And ultimately, because we never hear ourselves *express* opinions, our lack of intellectual self-esteem becomes self-fulfilling.

On top of this, the more we see of the world through the media, the more we begin to think of it as careening out of control. Unable to feel that our lives are part of history, we try to separate ourselves from what we perceive as chaotic and dangerous developments. This "survival mindset" makes us fearful and defensive. We begin to recoil from the world's conflict, only to find that the farther back we go, the more scared and unrelaxed we become.

However, if we believe that we are individuals whose thoughts and actions have repercussions for other people,

Your playing small doesn't serve you. There is nothing enlightened about shrinking.

Nelson
Mandela
(1994)

then morality enters the equation. None of us is truly happy if those closest to us are not. Our own goodness will be reflected back at us in the happiness of others. The goodness of others will inspire us further.

We have a choice. We can opt for self-contained individualism, belief in a world separated from mind and body, and in our own insignificance, which makes us fearful of such a world. Or we can opt for an integrated perspective, the influence of mind and body in perfect balance with the world's influence. Once we can see the world as *our* world, not *theirs*, and our selves as influential agents in the complex interplay of world, self and body, fear starts to drain away. Peace and harmony approach, like shy creatures to a hand that feeds them.

A little space within the heart is as great as this vast universe.

Upanishads
(c.800BC)

13

Perspectives on Stress

Stress is an over-used word. We often appear to vie with one another for the role of most stressed, and are gratified when people acknowledge the stress we are under. In fact, we tend to be so ready to boast about stress that we rarely stop to think where it comes from, and what it means about how we live.

The triggers of stress have evolved over time – our ancestors are unlikely to have had many problems with road rage! And surveys show that, while working conditions have greatly improved, we are working longer hours, and juggling ever more pressures in our work- and home-lives. Modern society expects us to be able to think quicker, work harder, excel at everything we attempt. In the name of civilized progress, we have given ourselves a modern condition, which we call stress.

In the face of perceived danger, we undergo immediate physiological changes. Hormone and adrenaline levels increase, diverting more blood to the brain and heightening sensual awareness. During spells of *everyday* stress, our body reacts similarly, but the alarm state (normally transmuted to fight or flight) is prolonged and, left unchecked, may cause physical or mental malfunction.

In Tibetan medicine, stress is related to an imbalance of the three "humours". Each humour, if present in excess, causes certain symptoms. So, if we suffer from "wind stress", our muscles tense up; "stress of the bile" brings impatience and irritability; "phlegm stress" gives rise to depression and fatigue. Few in the West subscribe to Tibetan views, yet the idea of the humours is interesting for the importance attached to balance. If we are out of balance (for example, our ambitions are out of balance with family life), then stress is a classic consequence.

Nothing in the affairs of men is worthy of great anxiety.

Plato
(c.429–c.347BC)

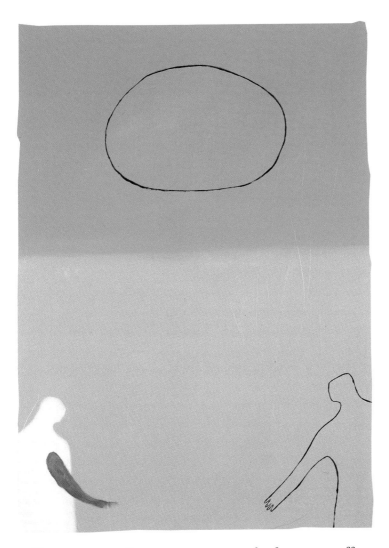

We often hear of people breaking down from overwork, but in nine cases out of ten they are really suffering from worry or anxiety.

Lubbock
(1834–1913)

The symptoms of stress vary enormously, from one sufferer to the next, and also in the range of specific triggers at work. Generally, stress is manifested as some kind of pain, which we may think of as bringing us a message: that something needs to change. Often, if we are stressed, a perfectly ordinary problem will seem insurmountable and the smallest of tasks will daunt us. One person may feel constantly tired, another will have phantom aches, while a third might fly into a rage (see pp.18–19 and 56–7). We do not need to be doctors to diagnose stress. Nor do we need special skills to treat it. If we can discover the real causes, then ultimately we can cure ourselves — so long as we never slip into the habit of regarding stress as a "natural" part of everyday life, or as a means to gain sympathy, or even praise.

The first step toward combatting stress is to accept that it exists as a result of our lifestyles or attitudes — it is not an indication of any inherent failures or shortcomings we may have. Increasingly, we are expected to be good at everything — not just at work and in the home, but also in the garden, when planning vacations, even while relaxing. We begin to expect so much of ourselves that the places we go and the things we do to unwind become triggers of stress in themselves.

We often hear people say that they work better "under pressure". If we consider the adrenaline curve, we might be tempted to find some truth in this. For a while, as adrenaline levels rise with gently increased pressure, performance may improve. However, once adrenaline production reaches a certain level, pressure inevitably turns into increasing amounts of stress, and the slope of the graph begins a sharp descent, until finally it reaches the point of breakdown. If we push ourselves *within* our limits, we may find success; if we push ourselves *to* our limits, we will certainly find stress.

Ultimately, we need to accept that, although life can be stressful, this is not one of its intrinsic characteristics. If we learn to understand our needs and capabilities, we can, in ways explored in this book, take control of stress. Nothing forces stress upon us: we can all keep this modern demon at bay.

Stress Ballooning

Exercise 1

This exercise is designed to help you to free yourself from habitual stress responses and to programme new responses to the situations that trigger your stress. Two balloons and a felt tip pen would be useful, but if you do not have access to them, do the exercise in your imagination.

1 What do you think are the triggers of your stress — work, a relationship, a change in domestic circumstances, worries about ageing? Rank the various stressors in order of severity.

2 Think about the most potent stressor. Remember your usual stressful response, and imagine you are blowing it into the first balloon.

3 Now take a large pin and burst the balloon. In the explosion, the old response has gone.

4 Take a second balloon and blow it up. Imagine positive energy filling it breath by breath. Write your new response on the balloon's surface.

5 What would your new action or thought pattern look like? Symbolize it visually on the balloon.

6 Tap the balloon gently into the air and keep it afloat a while as you fully absorb its message. Next time you face the situation, recall this balloon and the message you put on its surface.

Symptoms of Stress

*W*hen we feel stressed our predicament tends to be reflected in certain physiological and psychological symptoms, whose significance we may not fully understand. These are normal signs that we should re-evaluate our priorities – our body, or our state of mind, is telling us that something in our lives needs to change. Listed here are some of the tell-tale signs.

Loneliness We may feel isolated from friends and family, or have a lasting sense of being "lonely in a crowd".

Insecurity We may suddenly feel shy or exposed around people with whom we are usually filled with confidence. Or we may believe that we are always being judged or criticized.

Loss of concentration and memory We may find it hard to recall recent conversations or promises. We may often feel confused, so that understanding and retaining information could also be very difficult.

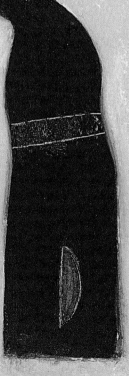

Not answering the telephone
We could lack interest in others, and fight off their concern.

Fatigue and sleeping difficulties Although we may feel constantly tired, we could also find it impossible to get to sleep.

Tears and mood swings One of the most common symptoms is that we cry easily. We may also be prone to mood swings — bouts of exhilaration alternating with dejection.

Impatience and irascibility We could find ourselves flying off the handle at any moment for trivial reasons; or we may snap at people, too quick to assume that they are accusing us.

Restlessness We could have difficulty sitting still over even short periods of time and we may fidget with our hands, twiddling our thumbs or playing with the rings on our fingers.

Obsessive working Treating work as a refuge can be a stress symptom, although stress can also manifest itself as absenteeism.

Compulsions We may find it difficult to avoid over-eating, or drinking, or smoking, or buying clothes. At the same time, our routines will become more rigid, and we will find it harder to do anything new.

Loss of appetite Food doesn't interest us any more. Either we don't eat, or we over-consume junk food, or whatever is in the store-cupboard or fridge.

Fear of silence Silence may cause us discomfort, so that we "over-talk" when with other people or leave on the radio or television when alone. Conversely, we may be intolerant of noise.

Appearance obsessiveness We may become excessively focused on our looks, exercising and dieting compulsively.

The Emotional Rodeo

*F*or centuries, the physiology and psychology of emotions have intrigued scientists, philosophers, and others who have been interested in forming a better acquaintance with the human mind. At a more mundane level lies the question: how should we deal with emotions? Should we allow them free rein, even though we know they may run counter to reason? Or should we bottle them up, at the risk of repressing something vital in ourselves? Aristotle (384–322BC), with typical moderation, believed that emotion should be expressed in the appropriate manner at the appropriate time. Cicero (106–43BC) held the view that emotion is a protective response, steering us away from harm and toward mercy.

Those who subscribe to the idea of the emotions being useful might point to the way in which they influence our effectiveness as agents acting upon our own lives and the world at large. When we experience happiness, we feel capable of anything; when we feel depressed, small tasks may seem beyond our capabilities. In the Ciceronian view of life, fear averts us from danger, sadness opens up our compassion. For most of us in the modern world, however, being unable to control our emotions is a cause of stress. If only we could learn to keep our feelings under a tight rein, we would feel more in control, then life would be so much easier.

We all, at certain times, experience surges of feeling that we are unable to suppress – the joy of reconciliation, or achievement of a long-sought goal; the sorrow of parting, or receipt of bad news.  However, there are two things that may make us suspect our emotions. First is the fact that we are emotionally suggestible. Movie-makers can

bring us to tears through imaginative manipulation of a story. We need only be introduced to a fictitious romantic couple, and we too become involved in the ups and downs of their relationship. In this way, we have *learned* to surrender our emotions to others. The second reason for mistrust is that emotions often stem from some baser, less graceful region of the self — the realm of jealousy, pride, anger, *Schadenfreude* (pleasure in another's misfortune).

We spend a great deal of time in combat with our emotions, trying either to suppress them or to prevent them from being apparent to the world. Indeed, it might be accurate to think of ourselves as riding an emotional rodeo, trying to keep our strongest feelings in the harness of reason, which is often perceived as the instrument of virtue.

In fact, to place emotion in opposition to reason is a recipe for unease. A more constructive approach is to filter out negative emotions, while admitting positive emotions freely past the censor into the world. Think of yourself as keeping a stable of wild horses, each of which has a tendency to sabotage your best efforts. At moments of intense feeling, you might hear the stable door banging as a horse attempts to escape. Try to envisage the first clattering noises from the stable as a warning signal to stop everything. If you are in the midst of a heated debate, halt the progress of the argument for a minute or so, and try to be calm. Bear in mind that your horses have been trained to respond to the exertion of human will, intelligence and reason. If you mentally order them to stay in their stalls, they will do so. It is only with your permission that they can break free. Try to imagine them quietly chomping their hay before you continue with the conversation in hand. Ideally, we should be able to silence the clamour of emotion if it becomes unhelpfully shrill, or if we recognize an underlying baseness – perhaps a sense that we are reverting to childish responses when our will is thwarted by someone else's reason. In order to maintain peace in our lives we have to become aware of our emotions, tuning ourselves in to their varying levels of interference to harness them at will.

There will be times, however, when we need to speak about our emotions – even if we are keeping them under lock and key. To talk intimately and emotively about what matters to us can be challenging for Westerners, and especially for men, who historically have been encouraged to be reticent. The problem is that when we speak of our feelings, it is as if they were being conjured into the open, in all their fury. Again, techniques of self-discipline are required. Imagine, for example, that the feelings you want to describe belong to someone else, and that the point of the exercise is for you to be a good witness, to help the course of justice. You must speak clearly and calmly, or the court will be confused, and will fail to understand the situation. Remember that you have chosen this moment for speaking your mind: your emotions often get the better of you, but now, for once, as you subject them to the analysis of reason, they are under your complete control.

Emotional Release

Presented below are simple, short term ways to release three of the most common negative emotions.

Anger *A natural response to anger is to clench our fists. In order to make this relaxing, pick a small, hard object, such as a stone, and place it in the palm of your hand. Squeeze the object as hard as you can and let go. Rock the object gently in your hand as if making peace with it.*

Sadness *With sadness comes lethargy and unresponsiveness. So, when you feel sad, take yourself for a walk. Focus your attention on the things that you pass. It doesn't matter where you go or how often you have done the same walk. With each step you take, you are working through your feelings of melancholy. Try to respond positively to sights, sounds and smells.*

Jealousy *When we feel jealous, our responses are similar to those of fear (jealousy often results from fear of loss). Our instinct is to fight, but instead of flying into a rage, gently run the fingers of one hand over the top of the other as if you were stroking a child's hand in comfort. Each stroke smooths away the emotion, and you should be able to respond more calmly.*

Worry

*C*lose your eyes for a moment and think about the things that have troubled you over the past week. How many are well-founded concerns, and how many unjustified worries?

There is a subtle difference between concern and worry. Concern is reasoned and purposeful, based on tracking a logic of cause and effect. We might shut all the windows before we leave the house, concerned that someone might break in, or that the wind might blow in and knock over a vase of flowers. Tracing the consequences of our actions upon others, we act diplomatically to avoid unnecessary harm or embarrassment. Through concern we avert discomfort, and hence gain the potential for feeling more relaxed.

Worry, on the other hand, lacks the logicality of concern. Instead, it tends to concentrate on pointless *wishing* that we could change the past, or on dwelling on unavoidable aspects of the future. Moreover, the mind becomes infected with free-floating anxieties, which accumulate and become habitual. We allow and often invite them to haunt us as a kind of regular "interference" pattern, which soon we begin to regard as normal. Specific problems may resolve themselves, but the anxious effects remain. Worry becomes a background buzz.

If we are listening to a slightly off-tune radio station for a 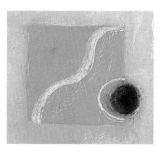 long time, and then adjust the dial to tune in accurately, we will be surpised at how much better the sound seems. Before we can fully relax, we must silence the point-lessly anxious hum of our lives, and tune in precisely to the pure silence where our personal quest for contentment may be fulfilled.

Silencing the Buzz

Exercise 2

Free-floating anxiety is, for many of us, a constant companion. We may have become so used to hearing the background buzz of worry that we do not even acknowledge its presence. This visualization exercise is designed to help you to identify this hum, and banish it — at least temporarily, until the next time worry starts to invade your outlook.

1 Sit comfortably and close your eyes. Imagine that you are walking down a path in a serene forest. Soon, you come across a clearing. Walk slowly to the centre of the glade and sit down.

2 As if from nowhere, animals surround you. They mean no harm, but each represents a concern. The larger the animal, the greater your anxiety. For example, a fleet-footed gazelle may represent a work deadline, a roaring lion, trouble within a relationship.

3 In one part of the glade is a beehive. Bees swarm near by, making the hum of free-floating worry.

4 Gently, touch each of the animals. As you do so, they quieten and disappear into the forest. The only sound left is the buzz of the bees.

5 Imagine all your tiny worries one by one entering the hive, until the glade is silent. Your worries are still, your concerns will be dealt with another day. All around is peace.

Guilt and Conscience

Our conscience is the receptacle of our moral wisdom, the source from which we take our ethical intuitions. An insistent alarm sounds here whenever we contemplate saying or doing something selfish, or cruel, or otherwise dubious. Like a severe but well-meaning friend, our conscience can be a harsh critic, re-running old movies of our behaviour, showing us how we acted badly or well, and giving us comprehensive notes on our performance, so that we might play our role better in the next scene.

A clear conscience never fears midnight knocking.

Ancient Chinese proverb

If we always listened to our conscience, we would steer ourselves through life contentedly, all the time notching up points for good behaviour. We would never put a foot wrong, and we would be at ease with ourselves. However, at one time or another, most of us fail to listen to our conscience. We strangle its voice and then experience a sinking feeling deep within us. The problem comes when we try to interpret this experience: should we acknowledge its validity or not?

There are two types of guilt — the emotion that the conscience secretes. The first type is *insightful guilt*, reminding us that we have performed or are contemplating something wrong, and that we had better take steps to remedy the situation if we are to regain peace of mind: we are losing ourselves, and can find our way back to our true course only by following conscience's signposts.

The other type of guilt is *programmatic guilt*, imposed from without. This is self-destructive. When we are children, our parents and teachers help to awaken in us an innate sense of right from wrong. Often, however, the influences brought to bear reflect a morality that we later reject as outmoded, or otherwise inappropriate. Worse, there might be forces at work

that use guilt as an instrument of power. The cliché of the bullying father, barking orders at his son like a sergeant-major, is one example: power becomes a substitute for intimacy, which the father's deep anxieties prevent him from expressing. Power-driven guilt of this kind is sustained only by fear. If guilt is persistently imposed by outside authority (school, family, religion, peer pressure), the voice of conscience becomes problematic. A counterclaim makes itself heard: aren't these guilt feelings the result of an *over*developed conscience? why shouldn't I be selfish for once?

How often do you feel that you adhere to the will of others because you fear the guilt of non-cooperation? If we are insecure, we may allow other people to manipulate our actions by "making" us feel guilty; but we feel still worse for failing to stand up for ourselves and neglecting to listen to our own inner voice. The collective, inherited conscience may be in the wrong; the personal, intuitive conscience in the right. We must learn to disentangle the two strands. In the process we build inner strength — the courage to resist external pressures that deep in our hearts we find ourselves unable to accept.

Everyone ought to bear patiently the results of his own conduct.

Phaedrus
(c. AD25)

Blame

*F*rom an early age we are taught that if we commit a misdemeanour, we will be held to account for it. Thus, we learn about error and culpability. At a fundamental level, these lessons are necessary for us to share in sustaining a safe, peaceable community. However, we often take the idea of culpability out of its social context, and apply it at a personal level. In the process we might introduce our own forms of error, perhaps blaming another for our own misjudgment. The "scapegoat", to whom blame is attached in order to absolve the guilt of a whole group, is a commonplace of psychology.

If we blame another person, we will often find ourselves in an atmosphere of "playground warfare": blame is passed back and forth like a tennis ball, and eventually the situation gets out of control, and the feelings aroused are out of all proportion to the situation. Factions may start to form — and factionism is the lowest form of politics. When we point the finger, three fingers point back at us.

Blame is wrong because at best it involves gross simplification, at worst a projection onto others of our own responsibility for error. As with any chronically negative response, its

effects are corrosive: blame destroys peace of mind by absorbing us in an unworthy project. To be able to find peace, we must first cultivate honesty (the courage to accept our own failings) and acceptance (the understanding that we have no control over the failings of others). Blame is an agitated reaction that can achieve no good result. It is an experience that has no place in the emotional repertoire of anyone who seeks relaxation.

Breaking the Chain of Blame

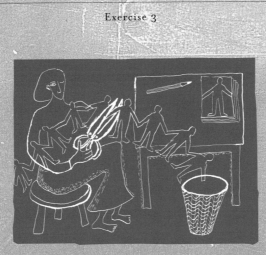

From time to time we might feel tempted to pass on the blame to someone else in apparent vindication of ourselves — even though at least some of the fault may lie at our own door. In this way we risk initiating a "chain of blame". Such chains are conduits for negative energy: it is always more constructive to break the chain, even though this might involve us in admitting more responsibility than we feel. The following questions provide a good basis from which you may evaluate any situation in which blame plays a part. Adapt them to suit your purposes.

1 What is the apparent cause of the conflict? Is there really something else at issue, beyond the ostensible reason? Perhaps there is an ulterior motive, driven by a grudge or jealousy? Can you break the blame chain by explaining this motive away?

2 If you are not the first in the chain of blame, why would others see fit to blame you? If you are not at fault, how might you diffuse the situation?

3 What would you lose if you accepted responsibility for the conflict? What is the worst-case scenario; what is the best? Would it matter if you failed to pursue your feeling of guiltlessness? Would your self-esteem suffer?

4 How might peace be declared? Can the whole issue that is at stake be sidestepped or ignored? What would happen if you proceeded as if the blame chain did not exist?

The Wheel of Fortune

*T*he traditional image of the Wheel of Fortune testifies to humankind's preoccupation with destiny in the way that we have envisaged the world: we rise to fall and fall to rise. A modern version of this idea is chance: we are at the mercy of randomness, and ill-fortune can strike at any time. We obtain not what we deserve, but what befalls us, by accident. If we feel vulnerable to chance, how can we be positive enough to relax?

Whether we believe in chance or in destiny (and many people still believe in destiny, as shown by their preoccupation with astrology, the Tarot and other "fortune-telling" devices), what is striking is the degree to which we are fatalistic. There are pros and cons in resignation: to accept things that happen and cannot be averted is a good thing; but to accept a fate that could be changed if only we had shifted ourselves into a different gear is a sad waste of our full potential.

O God! that one might read the book of fate, And see the revolution of the times.

William Shakespeare (1564–1616)

This is philosophy, but of a practical kind. To be able to relax, we need to have sketched out in our minds at least a rough-and-ready philosophy of life. A pragmatic approach, without any doctrinal or religious implications, is to strike a nicely judged balance, based on a realistic assessment of what we can and cannot control in our lives. We might think of this as steering a boat through hazardous waters. By applying our knowledge, skill and experience, we can hold our vessel on course and determine its direction, but only if we recognize the power of the ocean's currents and work with them rather than against them — ultimately we can control the boat, but we cannot control the swell of the sea. Accepting major mischances will take a great deal of endurance and courage; but accepting minor mischances is something in which we should all be able to school ourselves without too much difficulty.

Many of us all too readily equate chance with fortune, and so with money itself. Pursuing a financial or material fortune will not allow us to relax, because relaxation implies a balanced view of potential and limitation, not a feverish run for all we can get. To attempt to fulfil, to the utmost, every potential opportunity is to push ourselves beyond our limitations; what is more, it is a goal riddled with disappointment.

The notion of "opportunity cost", from economic theory, is relevant here. If we follow up a certain opportunity we inevitably incur the cost of leaving some parallel opportunity, unexploited. We shall never be able to go back and grab those forsaken chances. Contentment can come only if we embrace with commitment our chosen course of action, and look back without regret at the road we left unexplored.

Diligence is the mother of good fortune, and idleness, its opposite, never led to good intention's goal.

Cervantes
(1547–1616)

The Rock in the Stream

*I*n Daoist philosophy the river is a metaphor for life, which is in a constant state of flux. The flow is yielding, yet strong: it can carry huge boulders in its path, wear away a stony bank, and turn vast turbines. Nothing can halt the river's passage, because the water is always fluid enough to pass around any obstacle. In order to live a life of contentment, we can learn lessons from the river, gaining strength by the line of least resistance. In the words of the *Dao De Jing*, the classic collection of aphorisms that forms the basis of Daoism, "gentleness prevails over hardness".

Many people in modern times believe that the quickest route is the best: the faster we can complete one task, the sooner we can begin the next. We resemble not calmly flowing rivers, but swirling rapids, sending up angry white foam whenever they meet an obstacle. By the time we reach our goal, we are stale and spent, because we have striven so hard for success.

Daoists believe that humankind's attempted imposition of order on earth is a case of intellect vainly at war with nature. The result is stress. According to the natural order of things, a river, and anything that the river carries, will flow toward the sea. To achieve relaxation, we must *accept* life's natural flow (we *are* that flow), and allow ourselves to be borne along — not try to fight the current by swimming upstream, or willing the flow to move faster. If we surrender to the flow of the river, life will carry us where we want to go. This could take a little longer than we might have expected, and the experience may feel strange at first. Yet in time, by trusting the flow of the river, we will learn the art of acceptance. If we cease to struggle against the odds, our potential for growth is enlarged.

Wu Wei: the Art of Inaction

The idea that we can do nothing and allow matters to resolve themselves may sound like a recipe for escapism. Yet this is close to the Daoist principle of *wu wei*: action through inaction. Essential to *wu wei* is the avoidance of two things: exerting pointless effort, and contradicting nature, both of which are thought to lead to the opposite of the desired result and to a state of high tension.

Far from being escapist, following the Dao ("Way") involves abandoning strivings and tension in order to arrive at "creative quietude". "Whoever keeps in mind the great image of Oneness, the world will come to them. It will flow and not be violated, coming in calmness, oneness and blessedness." These and other aphorisms of the *Dao De Jing* make a fascinating theme for contemplation.

The Hand at the Tiller

*O*nce we have begun to accept life's flow, and to avoid point-less effort, we are letting go of our need to exert *control* — a much overvalued commodity, although one very much in tune with the temper of the times. We live in a society that has ele-vated control to the level of received doctrine. The ultimate arrogance of our species is to control nature itself, through genetic and environmental engineering. Eastern wisdom, increasingly accepted in the West as an oracle expounding bet-ter ways for us to live, concentrates on the more gentle idea of acceptance. This is not so much to do with fatalism; rather, it is a matter of working happily with, rather than stubbornly against, the grain of nature.

To find relaxation, we have to slow down. Life flows, it does not rush — despite exceptional episodes of accelerat-ed cause and effect. The most important undertakings are usually those that work out best when allowed plenty of time for completion. We all know what it feels like to have an idea that leaves us restless and dissatisfied until we have put it fully into effect. Such impatience undermines calm, in a way that illustrates an immutable law: will-power pitched against the grain of nature turns back harmfully against the agent.

There are times, of course, when it is appropriate to take decisive control over our lives: unless we have a hand at the tiller, our craft will drift miles from where we would like to be. At times we must be dogged about pursuing our goals. For example, we might be certain that we want to end a damaging relationship, against the other person's wishes. Think of the reverse situa-tion, however: there is a particular relationship that we want to *start*. Obviously, in such a case, all we can

do is set directions, and see if our *gentle influence* brings events to the desired outcome. We can nudge the tiller from time to time when we feel ourselves drifting off course. But a measure of doubt about where we are going is part of the adventure.

Relaxing in a limbo state, while unresolved issues surround various aspects of life, is the biggest challenge for many people. Anxiety focuses not around the issues themselves, but around the uncertainty of their outcome.

The best approach is probably to frame a set of statements about your situation that you find both true and comforting, and repeat them to yourself until they have the force of axioms. Bear in mind also that these periods of stasis, when we are *unable* to exert control, are moments of freedom. Farmers, who might spend the summer harvesting from morning till night, replenish their energy levels during the winter. We can all learn to identify the underlying patterns of natural relaxation in our lives.

Positive Thought

"*T*hink positive!" So often we are urged thus by others as we slide into the pessimism that makes relaxation impossible. But positive thinking is more than just an emotional rescue remedy: it is the source of our creativity and vision. Mahatma Gandhi's statement, "We have to be the changes we want to see in the world," is the simplest and fullest definition of positive thinking. This moves beyond the idea of transforming negative events into positive, like vinegar into honey: it is more to do with self-belief, the power of thought and the energy of optimism.

We cannot grow beautiful flowers if we have no soil. Our thoughts are our first creation, before we actually make any-thing, or change our surroundings, or alter the lives around us. If we don't trust or esteem our thoughts, we cannot easily believe in ourselves — even though we may attempt to establish false confidence by denigrating others. Respect for our own mind is the basis of positive thought, which leads to *peace of mind* — a deeply significant phrase, in which the connection between positive thinking and relaxation is made clear.

"To be the changes" is both to change and to effect change. The beauty of this idea lies in its holistic view of the self and the world. We bring about changes within ourselves at the same time that we transform the objects of our energies. And as we think our positive thoughts, we annihilate anxieties, in the way that a large wave annihilates smaller waves. Peace of mind is attained because we are wholly caught up in the positive thought processes that drown and silence all that is negative. Each of us is infinitely capable. If we think positively, our energy draws us toward success, like a magnet — all we have to do is believe in ourselves.

Using Hidden Riches

Most of us at some time or another will have had a really good idea about ourselves — one that seems an inspired, true insight about the way we want to be. Over a lifetime we may collect a number of these ideas, hoarding them, like precious coins, in a secret and secure place — our minds. By using this hidden wealth, instead of hoarding it pointlessly, we can banish a common cause of unease — the feeling that we are not realizing our full potential.

List your truest insights *about yourself, and determine that you will bring these insights to the light of day — where everyone will see the use you are making of them.*

Ask yourself *whether any of these insights can be used to abolish unnecessary tensions or contradictions in your life. Can they iron out anxieties and enable you to find peace if you heed their message?*

Believe in these ideas *as symbols of your essential character, rather than thinking of them as separate from yourself, a set of shining exceptions to the norm.*

Creative Visualization

*T*he mind is our own private cinema. The movies that it shows are of our own making: our conscious and unconscious minds serve as as co-directors. Across our interior screen, images from our past and hopes and fears for our future play themselves out in a never-ending extravaganza.

When the images are free to drift, these movies are our dreams or daydreams. But we all have the power to control the imagery, by consciously drawing upon two resources: the visual imagination; and the discipline that enables us to channel that imagination by excluding whatever we deem irrelevant. This is the essence of "creative visualization", which may be used in various ways to bring us closer to peace of mind.

At the one end of the spectrum, the technique provides a "soft" route to relaxation: we become lost in the landscape of our own imagining, and as we do so we relinquish our preoccupations. Also, we can use creative visualization as a method of goal-setting (see pp.82–3): by envisaging our ambitions, we make them tangible and thus strengthen motivation. More interestingly, we can use similar means to work on our moods or perceptions, exploiting the power of suggestion and symbol, as in many of the exercises in this book.

When we are children, our imaginations are at their most fertile. As we grow older, we become more preoccupied with "real" life, and in the process forget that fanciful creations of the mind can give simple pleasure. Often, if the imagination works at all, it is the servant of pessimism: what would happen if I lost my job? What if my husband left me tomorrow? Creative visualization is, by definition, positive. Banishing the bleak scenario, we conjure images that enable us to see our situations, even our very identities, constructively.

An Imaginary Balloon Ride

Exercise 4

This visualization should bring about a more relaxed mood. Record yourself reading it aloud, slowly, clearly and softly. Elaborate the story with your own images. Then, sitting comfortably, set the tape running and close your eyes. Conjure up each image as vividly as possible.

1 You are walking along a country lane. The sun beats down on your head and shoulders. To your left is a beautiful forest; to your right, a field, into which you turn. Ahead of you is a hot-air balloon ready for flight.

2 You approach the balloon and step into the basket. The balloon begins to rise very slowly. As you look down, you can see a village, a lake, some mountains. When you look at the sky, you see a bird glide past you. There is absolutely no noise. Silently you rise higher and higher.

3 Beneath you everything becomes a swirl of blue and green. You can see no borders or boundaries, just one world, as you have never fully realized before. As you understand this, the balloon begins its descent.

4 The details gradually return into view and the balloon comes to rest in the middle of the field. You step out of the basket, walk down the path through the village to the lake that you could see from the air. The water on the lake is absolutely calm and still — just how you yourself feel.

39

Stillness, Breath and Calm

*B*reathing is our most fundamental interaction with our world. An unbroken rhythm, it connects us with every living thing through a perfectly balanced exchange of carbon dioxide and oxygen. To breathe is our most natural instinct, but one that many of us have forgotten how to perform properly. Re-learning the correct way to breathe can have untold benefits for our health and well-being.

The way we breathe — shallowly or deeply, rapidly or slowly, smoothly or abruptly — is a barometer for our physical and emotional state, and one of the first indicators of whether or not we are suffering from stress. We all know that proper breathing oxygenates the blood and allows the voice its full range of expression, but less obvious is the power of breathing over the mind: sending healthy, bright red blood to our brain is the best basis for calm, methodical, considered thinking. Furthermore, long, smooth exhalations can help in easing minor physical aches and tensions — it can seem that they are almost literally being blown away. Simple, wholesome breathing techniques can help too in the relief of anxieties.

If we are not able to breathe properly, we cannot fully relax our bodies and minds. How well we feel is closely bound up with how well we breathe.

Breath and Emotion

*I*magine holding a jar in each hand. One jar is full of coffee and the other appears to be empty. In monetary terms the jar of coffee seems the most valuable. But the second jar is full of air, the most precious substance of all, and also the one that we most take for granted. When we think about how we breathe and its benefits for relaxation, it is important to remember that we cannot live by air alone, but neither can we live without it. Air is the priceless gift of nature.

Most people use their lungs to their full potential only when they laugh or cry deeply, and both these experiences bring in their wake a release of emotional tension, so that we feel relaxed and relieved. Sadness, regret or exhaustion usually express themselves in a sigh — a long, slow exhalation.

The way that we breathe reflects our emotional disposition, because breathing and feeling are intimately connected. The main causes of abnormal breathing are stress, distress and strong feeling. When we are angry, we might hold our breath. Nervousness causes short, shallow breaths and yawning. Relaxed breathing, on the other hand, is moderate, slow and rhythmic, and feels natural and easy, when we think about it. But we hardly ever do: it is automatic. Yet most people most of the time unconsciously impede the full extent of their breath.

One way to envisage the effects of unnatural breathing is by comparison with the wind. A tempestuous gale can have devastating effects upon nature. The longer it lasts, the more extensive the damage to trees and shrubs. Even after the wind has abated, the aftermath in the countryside may take some time and a great deal of care to recover. So it is with our own well-being. When our breathing is uncalm, we hyperventilate ("over-breathe"). Too much carbon dioxide is taken out of the

bloodstream, causing dizziness, faintness, panic attacks, sweating, and other disturbing physical and psychological symptoms. Unfortunately, abnormal breathing can outlive the emotion that caused it, so that it becomes a nervous habit. When this happens, even slight unease triggers hyperventilation as a stress response.

However, if the way we breathe is a symptom of emotional extremity, then it is also the cure. By learning to breathe evenly and deeply, and by practising regularly, we can begin to make the most of the gift of air. This in turn will help us to relax, even during times of heightened emotion. Eventually, we will find that relaxed breathing becomes habitual, allowing us to concentrate on relaxing our mind.

The Breathing Bias

*W*e tend to breathe using one of two main muscle groups. In chest (costal) breathing, the ribcage lifts upward and outward, and the air enters the upper rather than the lower part of the lungs. In abdominal (diaphragmatic) breathing, the diaphragm contracts, so that air may enter the lower lungs.

Chest breathing is useful after exercise, when the body has an urgent need for oxygen. However, breathing in this way during sedentary periods requires a great deal of unnecessary effort and fails to draw oxygen into the lower lung, which is most abundantly perfused with blood. Costal breathing is the natural response to stress, and unless consciously controlled can cause persistent over-breathing (see pp.42–3).

Abdominal or diaphragmatic breathing is preferable when the body is quiescent. The contraction of the diaphragm requires minimal energy expenditure and improves the ventilation in the lower part of the lungs. Babies and children naturally breathe in this way, but, for many reasons, in adulthood we forget diaphragmatic breathing. If we can apply ourselves to re-learn this important skill, we will begin to feel more relaxed in body and mind.

You can determine your breathing bias by lying on your back on the floor. If, as you naturally breathe in, your chest rises, your bias is costal breathing; if your abdomen rises, your bias is diaphragmatic. Whichever your bias, it is always beneficial to practise relaxed, diaphragmatic breathing. Adopt a comfortable position, and breathe out in one long, slow exhalation. Once you feel that your lungs are empty, breathe in again, but take special care to make sure that it is your abdomen that rises. Exhale completely. Spend ten or fifteen minutes each day breathing purposefully in this way.

Breathing to Defeat Stress

Make a list *of the times during the day when you tend to feel least relaxed. Your stress may be triggered by a place, a person or an event. Carefully judge each daily activity in terms of stress levels. You may need to think about this over a few days — take as long as you need, and each time you are able to identify a particular "stressor" (trigger of stress), note it down. Also, make a list of forthcoming events that you feel especially anxious about.*

Devise visual reminders *and place them strategically. You might decide to draw a star on some cards, placing them where you will see them at the times of stress on your list. If your times include travelling or walking down a busy street, you could use, say, your thumb or ring finger as your trigger. Decide on the prompt and concentrate on it for a few minutes to fix it as a reminder. This may sound silly, but your mind will readily accept the mental nudge.*

Breathe deeply *and evenly whenever your prompts are brought to your attention.*

Imagine that your tension *is released for ever. Eventually, you won't need reminding to begin relaxed breathing — it will become natural, even at times of stress.*

Unlocking Breath

*B*reathing is sharing — we all breathe the same air. When we are upset, it can seem that our breath is dammed up, just as our emotions are, by the inhibitions that prevent us from expressing them. We brace our bodies, clip our speech and give short gasps. If we let air out (share it), we will liberate ourselves from our store of pain. On exhalation comes release — the sob, cry or shout that we fear giving way to. Try a simple experiment. Tense your muscles as if in response to danger, then release them, imagining that the threat has gone. Did you hold your breath and then release it? For most of us this reaction is so normal that it doesn't even flicker into consciousness.

The pressure of emotion is difficult to hold in for too long. Dammed up behind closed doors, it surges until the doors give way, and we may then experience an overwhelming rush of feeling. We might burst into tears or explode with anger. If we do so, our breath is released in erratic bursts, leaving us breathless and often voiceless. Having let go, we may feel exposed and vulnerable, and then we experience some of the most unrelaxing emotions of all — embarrassment, regret, guilt or shame.

In extreme situations, we may even have a panic attack in which our airways feel blocked, so that it is almost as though we are being strangled. This usually happens after a build-up of anxiety — and we may have become so used to this anxiety that we have not noticed its full extent. In such a situation, although correct breathing may seem quite a challenge, one way to combat the attack is to concentrate on breathing deeply. Imagine that the air is clearing away the blockage. With each breath, more air is able to filter through, until finally our breaths become deeper and our body is able to relax again.

Sometimes the panicky feeling of locked breath is suddenly triggered by a deep-seated fear. Someone afraid of flying might have this experience at the point of take-off. Someone who is claustrophobic may start to panic and over-breathe as soon as the elevator door closes. It can take many years to overcome a phobia, and many different techniques have been used, with varying levels of success. One sufferer might, for example, choose to see a hypnotist. Another might gradually build up his or her confidence, by first contemplating the feared situation, then simulating it, then confronting it. But whatever approach we might take to our phobia, we can always benefit from concentrating on our breathing. If we practise setting free our breath, imaginatively associating this action with the release of fear, then breathing will begin to provide both a focus and a respite in times of panic.

When we dam up our breath, we not only repress our emotions and fuel our panic, but also we strangle our voice. As the voice teacher Patsy Rodenburg has observed, "Without proper breathing, our connection to language flounders."

Reduced vocal competence comes hand in hand with unrelaxed breathing. If we find it hard to get our words out, we might find ourselves either stuttering them, or spilling them forth in an uncontrolled jumble, one word becoming indistinguishable from the next. Alternatively, our voice might become unnaturally high-pitched or unusually hoarse. Indeed, if we are extremely scared or intimidated, we might lose our voice altogether.

Most people have, at one time or another, experienced the loss of vocal power that accompanies periods of anxiety. In a less severe form, this "strangled voice" syndrome can occur every day as a result of self-doubt. Our voices become reedy and limp because our breathing becomes more shallow. Speech comes in fits and starts, and we lose volume and distinction at the ends of our sentences, to the point where statements may even begin to sound like questions. This loss of resonance further undermines our conviction in what we are saying, and soon others begin to lack confidence in us too. Altogether, we have set out on a journey toward increasing anxiety and self-doubt.

However, before we can start to release our voices from strangulation, we must become practised at unlocking our breath, by breathing more deeply and healthily. The exercise on the opposite page combines meditation with breath control to this end. Practise it as often as you can.

The Air Meditation

Exercise 5

This simple meditative breathing exercise will help you to re-establish calm breathing. It is a good first-aid exercise to see you through difficult emotional situations. It will provide you too with the basis for recovering full vocal control.

1 Sit or recline in a quiet room with your eyes closed. Visualize your thoughts as a mass of bubbles. Exhale slowly through your mouth. As you do so, imagine all these thought-bubbles being blown away. You already begin to feel more relaxed.

2 Now re-direct your entire attention to your nostrils. Breathe in and out through your nose, and as you do so visualize the air passing through the nostrils at your beck and call.

3 Concentrate hard on producing a long, smooth exhalation, letting the inhalation take care of itself.

4 If your mind starts to wander, don't give up. Simply re-focus your attention on your nostrils and try to let the sensation of breathing fill your consciousness.

5 Practise this exercise for as long as is comfortable. Repeat it daily until you feel yourself breathing naturally.

Speech, Breath and Relaxation

*O*nce we have learned – or, rather, re-learned – how to breathe properly (see pp.44–9), we can begin to understand how vocalization can be used to promote calm.

A powerful voice need be neither loud nor forceful. When a handful of stones is thrown carelessly into a pool, water splashes in all directions, and anyone close to the shore will flinch from getting wet. However, if a single small stone is dropped carefully, it will gently disturb the surface of the water, sending out ever-increasing circles, whose perfect symmetry and gentle motion will encourage passers-by to stop and watch. Every sound we hear is like a single stone dropped into water. The waves that sound makes in the air are concentric circles radiating out in all directions. If the sound is loud, that is because the vibrations in the air are fast and erratic. A pleasant, well-modulated sound might be imagined as resonating through the air to create waves of relaxation that wash over anyone who is listening.

Such invisible waves of calm may also be used to dispel our own anxieties. The Sanskrit word *mantra* means "speech". During meditation a mantra is used to focus the mind, allowing ripples of sound gently to wash away external anxiety and encircle the meditator in a profound state of relaxation.

A mantra is also useful for cleansing away a specific anxiety. Think about the factors that tend to make your voice lose its resonance – a particular situation, perhaps, that has made you feel nervous in the past. By controlling your voice in one resonant sound, you can visualize this stress trigger dissolve as the gentle waves lap it away. The exercise opposite will guide you step by step through this method: follow it to experience a gradual dissolution of anxiety.

In Indian belief, the "Om" (shown here) is the mula mantra, the "root" syllable. The vibrations of its sound are thought to have created the gods.

Breath Mantras

Exercise 6

In difficult situations our voices show our anxiety. Intoning a mantra can help to steady the tone of your voice, so that when you next have to speak during stress, you will do so with greater confidence. In essence this is an aural form of meditation.

1 Consider how your voice tends to react when you are experiencing strong emotions. For example, it might rise to a higher pitch.

2 Choose a simple sound that will help you back to vocal stability. The sound "om" will correct high-pitched tones by inviting a low, resonant delivery.

3 Sit with your back straight. Focus on breathing out through your nose. Allow your breathing to settle into a smooth, regular rhythm.

4 Now visualize your tense situation in symbolic form. So, for example, a fear of strangers might be represented by a dark silhouette.

5 Don't wait for the fear to take root. As soon as you have chosen your symbol, intone your chosen mantra, repeating it with every exhalation.

6 Allow every repetition to dissolve the image in your mind. Imagine that the sound of the mantra transforms your fear into dust and your breathing blows the dust away for ever.

Sensual Enhancement

*B*reath and breathing are pilot and co-pilot of one of our most important senses: smell. Close your eyes for a moment and breathe in deeply through your nose. Concentrate on the smells that you detect. What mental images or states of mind do they conjure up? Most of us have walked down the street and passed a stranger wearing the same perfume or aftershave as someone we have known and liked. Immediately, the emotions that we felt for that person come flooding back.

Arguably, of all the five senses, smell has the most subtle and insidious impact upon us. Certain aromas have particular influence over our moods. Citrus, pepper and freshly ground coffee tend to be invigorating and uplifting; whereas warm, fresh-baked bread, wood smoke and aromatic teas are soothing and conducive to contemplation.

The effect of smells will be personal to each of us, reflecting our unique blend of past experiences. A smell that we find

relaxing or uplifting, perhaps because it triggers happy memories, might mean nothing to a friend. One aspect of the quest for relaxation is to seek out the smells that help us feel most contented and calm. Through experiment, we might find an oil, soap or fragrance that reminds us of a blissful time in childhood, or of a dear friend or loved one.

On a more physical level, our sense of smell can help us to concentrate on, and enjoy to the full, our breathing. Once we have identified a pleasurable aroma, long, profound breaths will offer us the deepest satisfaction, as breath and scent mingle in an intimate duet of fulfilment.

Aroma-soothing

Exercise 7

We all know how soothing a scented bath can be, or a room filled with the fragrance of essential oils. However, we tend to rely on the labels of bottles to guide our choice toward the most appropriate aroma, forgetting that our own sense of smell is the best guide of all.

1 Throughout the day, try to become aware of the many and various smells that surround you. As you become conscious of a smell, ask yourself what associations it has for you. What other sense impressions, if any, does it conjure up?

2 Isolate a few smells that you find calming. These need not be obvious – you might, for example, find the smell of burning wood comforting and the smell of lilies cloying. There are no orthodoxies – the smells that you find most soothing are likely to be particular to you.

3 Seek out one of these smells (you might find appropriate aromatherapy oils, or else find them in nature). Sit or lie quietly, focusing on the smell to amplify it in your perception.

4 Now become aware of your breathing. Breathe from your abdomen and not your chest: this way, your breathing will be deep and calming and you will fully appreciate your aroma. Think of the aroma as a relaxant that you draw into the centre of your being with every inhalation. Blow out your stress with every exhalation.

The Body at Rest and in Motion

*M*any of us believe that exercise eases physical and mental tensions: after a vigorous session of swimming, or cycling, or working out, or ball sports, we feel pleasantly exhausted, able at last to relax in a chair or on the ground or floor without feeling that our energies are bundled in a knot, preventing our body from benefiting fully from this brief interlude of inaction. However, to achieve a true state of bodily relaxation, it should not be necessary to exhaust ourselves like this. There are various simple techniques, including meditation, postural adjustments, muscular stretches and massage, that can be used to smooth out the physical symptoms of mental tension. The senses, particularly smell and touch, can also be brought into play with beneficial effects. By accurately applying these bodily solutions, many of them based on Eastern relaxation methods, we help ourselves to attain a true stasis of the mind. At the same time, we can improve the efficacy of physical relaxation techniques by reinforcing them with easy-to-follow mental disciplines. As in all aspects of well-being, the physical and the mental are holistically conjoined, and cannot be separated without some sacrifice of personal fulfilment.

Tension Traits

*F*reeze! The way we sit, stand or walk down the street can speak volumes about our state of mind. If your body, in this frozen moment, were a sculpture, what messages would it transmit? Every attitude and expression tell a tale about personality and our circumstances; every posture is a song about our feelings.

The pseudo-science of body language suggests that the body doesn't lie. This is not to say, however, that we can't hide the uncomfortable *physical* sensations of the body. For example, if we have a headache we can usually make it through a meeting without wincing in pain every time someone speaks. But, if we feel nervous, bored or emotionally uncomfortable, our tension traits (such as tapping, nail biting and hair twiddling) will begin to transmit the messages that our tact or circumspection prevents us from voicing out loud.

Each tension trait is thought to have a particular meaning. We tap to restrain and divert ourselves from more overt action, such as walking out of a room because we are bored. We bite our nails to deflect our destructive instincts. And we fiddle with our hair because, when we feel chastised or in need of comfort, we tend to revert to baby behaviour, invoking the period of minimal responsibility.

So, if we are not consciously aware of the messages of our body language, how do we go about supressing our tension traits, and ultimately breaking the habits that they have become? The first step toward freedom from our habits is not, as folk wisdom suggests, to bind our hands so that we can't bite our nails: it is to raise our own awareness of the circumstances that trigger our unrelaxed feelings. We have to learn to become our own spectators. As soon as we see ourselves reach for our "security blanket", we have identified one of perhaps many

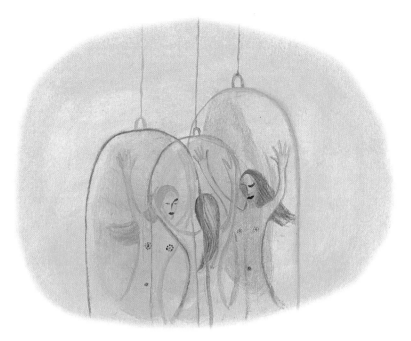

situations that trigger our anxiety. Thus begins the route to self-knowledge, the process by which we discover, one by one, the deep sources of our tensions within ourselves.

One technique, after an encounter that leaves us feeling unrelaxed, is to run an imaginary video from the point of view of one of the other people involved (it is mostly other people who set off our tension traits). What image of us would that witness have experienced? Our first guesses, even if we hesitate to acknowledge their validity, are usually accurate.

By identifying a tension trait's true cause, we rationalize the problem. Then we can work at uprooting the cause and letting go of the symptom. In the shorter term, techniques such as muscle release (see pp.64–5), massage and yoga are helpful for inducing physical serenity, as groundwork to prepare for anxious episodes. Once we have reached a physical state of relaxation, we will be better equipped to begin the interior journey of self-discovery on which lasting calm depends.

Rest and Sleep

*S*leep performs two main functions. First, it allows our physical body to regenerate itself through inactivity; and second, it permits dreams to carry out their mysterious exploration of our unconscious (see pp.134–5).

During sleep, we continually ascend and descend through four levels of consciousness. Stage 1, the lightest sleep, is characterized by dreaming; Stage 4, the deepest, is significant for its lack of dreams and almost complete oblivion to external stimuli. Typically, Stage 1 sleep lasts between five and twenty minutes, and occurs every ninety minutes or so. These periods increase in length throughout the night.

But is dreamful sleep (D-sleep) more or less restful than non-dreamful or synchronized sleep (S-sleep)? There are no hard and fast answers to this question, as sleep theory is still in its infancy. What is clear is that each of us enjoys a personal sleeping cycle, the time we spend asleep varying widely from one individual to the next. The key to quality sleep is being able to identify our natural sleeping pattern and then adhere to the required quota as much as possible.

Many of us rarely let our sleeping cycle take its natural course. As we work longer hours and fill our time with more activity, we stay up later to give ourselves "quiet time" before going to bed; or we force ourselves to stay awake to catch the end of a TV movie or to spend more time talking to our partner. We further upset our natural rhythm by using an alarm clock – quite literally frightening ourselves out of sleep.

Restful sleep is vital for relaxation. Without it we force our minds and bodies to work against nature, which can only lead to fatigue and greatly increased anxiety.

The Sleep Experiment

Exercise 8

Making sure that we get the right amount of sleep is no less important than eating when we are hungry and drinking when we are thirsty. This exercise will help you to find your own sleeping cycle, which you can then follow as a programme for health and well-being.

1 Mentally prepare yourself for sleep. Register the fact that between now and the moment you drift off, nothing can hinder your calm thoughts. Banish any nagging worries by meditating on the strengthening sleep ahead.

2 Go to bed when moderately tired. Make a note of the time. Listen to gentle music, read a soothing book or do another meditation just before sleep. Don't set your alarm; instead, sleep until you awaken naturally. Make a note of the time when you become fully awake. How long did you sleep?

3 Repeat this exercise for as many nights as it takes for the pattern of your sleeping and waking to become broadly regular. This is your natural and most restful sleep cycle.

4 If you have to wake up at a specific time, make sure nothing deters you from going to bed when you feel tired (for example, ask friends not to call after a certain time). Try to wake less abruptly — for example, you could ask your partner to rouse you gently; or you might consider an alarm clock that plays soft music.

Achieving Stillness

Yoga is the Sanskrit word meaning "union" or, more literally, "yoke". Once a single orthodox system of Indian belief, yoga has developed into four main forms. Hatha Yoga aims to unite body and mind through postural discipline, to make the body worthy of receiving the spirit; Karma Yoga unites good deeds with material release; Bhakti Yoga unites the yogin (practitioner) with an object of devotion through prayer; and Raja (meaning "royal" or "kingly"), the highest form of yoga, unites the yogin with the creator or "source" by purifying spiritual and mental energy.

The aim of all types of yoga is to free the yogin of his or her ties with the material world in order that he or she may return to the original, ecstatic state, known as *samadhi*. The senses must be numbed; and consciousness must be detached from *maya*, the "world of illusion". Once self-realization is brought about in this way, the conscious mind experiences the self as soul or spirit. This can only be achieved through deep concentration, to the point at which the mind becomes completely still. Once re-united with the "source", the yogin feels deeply and blissfully happy.

The *asanas* ("seats" or "postures"), with which yoga is often typically associated, are most characteristic of Hatha Yoga.

These positions are meant to cleanse the body so that it may experience re-birth into a state worthy of receiving spiritual enlightenment.

Yoga and meditation go hand in hand with one another. However, at the ultimate stage of yogic development, the practitioner moves beyond awareness of meditation to become a fully spiritual being.

The "Limbs" of Yoga

Exercise 9

*Raja Yoga has eight "limbs" or stages. The first five train the body to make it worthy
of receiving the spirit; the final three deal with creating the perfect self. This exercise takes
you through all the stages: do it for as long as you feel comfortable.*

1 Spend the day finding relaxation through moral good. Be honest, faithful and self-disciplined. These are the *yama* and *niyama* limbs.

2 In a quiet room, sit comfortably (*asana* limb). You do not have to choose a traditional yogic posture, simply one that will allow you to remain still for as long as possible.

3 Breathe evenly and deeply (*pranayama* limb), so that your abdomen rises as you breathe in. Exhale slowly. In this way the body and mind are calmed.

4 Withdraw your attention from your surroundings. Turn your senses inward (*pratyahara* limb).

5 In your imagination picture a colourful circle or spiral. Concentrate on it for a while (*dharana* limb).

6 Imagine that your energy is flowing into this image. Make this the focus of your meditation (*dhyana* limb). Do this for as long as possible. (*Samadhi* limb is a trance-like state, where the yogin has become unaware even of meditation, but fully aware of the spiritual self.)

The Fitness Paradox

*E*xercise has come to be regarded as the secret of being healthy and attractive. We find ourselves going to the gym in our lunch hours; attending exercise classes after work; playing sport at the weekends; and following fitness videos at home. For those of us who adhere to its regime, exercise consumes enormous amounts of time and energy; for those of us who don't, "exercise guilt" can become an arm-chair obsession, undermining our self-esteem.

Given that we know that guilt is stressful (see pp.26–7), we might think that the exercise road is the better route to take. Indeed, most fitness enthusiasts contend that they hold the key to relaxation, that exercise provides a dependable way to release tension and stress. To a certain extent this is true: adrenaline levels increase with exercise, initially improving performance. However, the paradox lies in the fact that push-ing our bodies during strenuous activity fatigues our muscles and starves them of oxygen. The body releases harmful lactic acid into the muscle to make up the oxygen shortfall. This fundamental deficiency eventually forces us to relax because we are physically exhausted. But there is nothing worthy or ben-eficial about becoming tired in this way – it is against nature to force our bodies to cope with insufficient oxy-gen combined with increased levels of toxins.

For many people the fitness paradox and the beauty myth are closely allied. Pseudo-logic dictates that "if I look after my body, I will become attractive; if I am attractive, I will be more successful personally and pro-fessionally; if I am more successful, I will be happy." Certainly, exercise can make us feel better, and is a way of maintaining the temple that houses the spirit. At a

more mundane level, there are obvious medical and psychological benefits in staying supple, preventing obesity, and generally keeping ourselves in trim. However, we do not need to thrash our bodies to the limit to reap the rewards of fitness. Stepping off the exercise treadmill, we might consider a less dynamic recreation in which both mind and body can contribute to a sense of release, freedom and relaxation. Walking, swimming and slow cycling, for example, invite mind and body to play together rather than to work apart.

For true, holistic well-being, the health of the inner self must be given as much attention as our physical condition. If we neglect the mind's welfare, we become tense and pale, even seriously unwell. There is little point in maintaining the temple if the sanctuary inside is in ruins.

Muscle Release

*W*e know that when the mind feels uneasy, the body uses its own language to convey symptoms of stress (see pp.56–7) that disclose our hidden feelings. Over time, our persistent mental attitudes become fixed in our muscles (a habit of thought becomes a habit of posture), the tension building up in our limbs causing stiffness and discomfort.

Exercise can be an effective release for the stiffness caused by falling asleep in an awkward posture, but is useless at resolving habits of stiffness accumulated through our mental and emotional responses. The fact is that mind over body created this tension, so mind over body must abolish it.

Think about the flexibility that a baby or toddler enjoys. There are very few adults who can still put their toes in their mouth, or who find it easy to curve their back in such a way as to form a "bridge" (hands and feet on the floor, back arched, stomach stretched toward the ceiling). As we grow, we pick up and collect moments of tension – parental rows, difficulties at school, adolescent pangs, leaving home for the first time, the first job, the first relationship, and so on. Although many of these episodes may seem to have been forgotten, the physical and mental tension that they created at the time of their occurence is stored up in our muscles, causing us to stiffen. To release such stiffening we need to take purposeful remedial action.

Often, we are so used to feeling tense that we are not alerted by the messages that our body sends us. But we can re-alert our minds and set free the tension in our muscles by following the exercise opposite. As each muscle is released from tension, the mind's burden lightens.

The Dissolved Body

Exercise 10

Over the years our attitudes can become like rock, hardening themselves against a genuine response to life's changes. Sometimes we need to give ourselves time to become loose again — not to feel life's pressures more acutely, but to deal with them more effectively.

1 Lie comfortably in a warm room with your eyes closed. Allow your body and mind to slow down for a minute or two, by remaining still and quiet.

2 Keeping your eyes closed, take your attention to the toes of one foot. Clench them tightly for about five seconds, then relax them. Do this twice more. As you clench and relax in this way, imagine that your toes are turning to liquid, which then gently flows around you. Now clench and relax the other foot, turning that to fluid in the same way.

3 Continue to work progressively up your body, tensing and releasing. Do your shins, then your thighs, buttocks, stomach, chest, back, hands, forearms, upper arms, shoulders, neck, jaw, cheeks, eyes and brow.

4 Your whole body should now be free to flow. You visualize this, while keeping your attention focused in the centre of your forehead.

5 Now try to tense and relax the movement in your mind: let your thoughts float to the surface and watch them dissolve and flow away.

The Gateway of Touch

We've touched a thousand ways, like summer leaves touching.

Anonymous Chinese poem

*W*hen we are babies, touch is probably the most comforting of our senses. Held against our mother's body, we are contented and reassured; feeling her hand softly stroking our cheek, we are quietened. But as we grow older we tend to "lose touch", seeking fewer cuddles and kisses, even becoming embarrassed by skin contact. By literally separating ourselves from family and friends, we suppress an instinctive need to communicate and be relaxed through touch.

Studies show that people who have pets suffer less from stress-related diseases, such as high blood pressure and heart disease, than those who don't. The reason is largely down to touch. When we stroke a pet, we comfort and relax the animal. The gentle rhythm of our stroking, and the pleasure of the pet's contented reaction, conspire to relax us.

This is not necessarily to say that we need to begin stroking other people in order to find relaxation. But think about the most tender moments in your adult life. Perhaps you will recall a hug from a friend, or your partner running a finger over your cheek, or someone taking your hand to reassure you. We all give and receive touch from time to time, yet we have forgotten its benefits. We are so used to seeing touch in a family context, or linked with sex, that we tend to undervalue its efficacy as a simple, reassuring act of connection between two people.

The gateway of touch need not be opened only by those who know each other intimately. Consider the impression that your handshake may have on someone. A warm, strong handshake inspires the other person's confidence and trust in you. Sensing this, you will enjoy renewed confidence in yourself, and so will begin to feel more at ease.

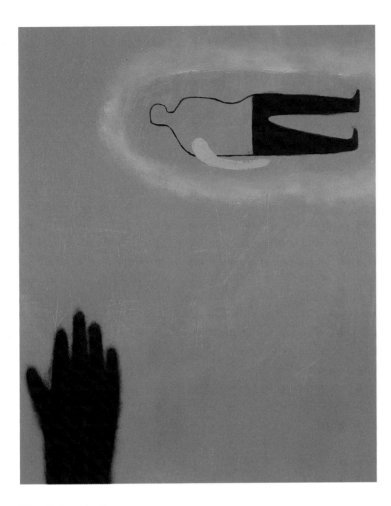

*Saints have hands
that pilgrim's
hands do touch,
And palm to palm
is holy
palmists' kiss.*

William
Shakespeare
(1564–1616)

The Palmist's Kiss

Imagine that you are filled with fast-flowing, positive energy. With a partner or a close friend, make a "palmist's kiss". Sit opposite one another and press your left palm to his or her right palm, and your right palm to their left. Close your eyes and imagine the flow of energy — warm and invigorating — passing through your palms and coursing through your body. Interlock fingers and squeeze gently in reassurance. Imagine that the energy has cleansed your body of all fear.

The Gift of Hands

*T*he power of touch provides the basis for spiritual healing practices all over the world. In many cultures the laying on of hands represents a transference of healing energy — an idea expressed through a wide range of disciplines, from the Japanese tradition of *shiatsu* (see pp.72–3) to faith healing.

However, we do not need to believe in a particular healing or mystical discipline to benefit from the gift of hands. In many respects, our hands enjoy the pleasure of most of our physical contact with other people, and with things. Simply using them to rub or to stroke — call it massage if you will — can release our tension and so simultaneously repair and relax both body and mind.

The power of massage lies not just in the physical sensations for both masseur and subject, but in the care and re-assurance that it communicates between two people (see pp.66–7). In a day-to-day context, sensual touching has become too readily confused with sexuality, and we have become introverted and resistant to physical contact, conscious that touch can be mis-interpreted. There is nothing erotic about massage: it is a rich combination of mind and body as they work together to find peace. When we give a sensitive, gentle and thoughtful mas-sage, we express our acceptance of and respect for another person — we literally handle them with care.

Don't imagine that you have to receive a massage in order to benefit from the gift of hands. Applying one can be just as restorative. If, as masseur, we can learn to concentrate our attention solely on the task in hand, and be calmed by the rhythm of our strokes, we can release our minds of mundane concerns. At the same time, our generous absorption in relax-ing another person is itself a source of positive energy.

Drawing the Face

Exercise 12

Most of us find it hard to close our eyes and create a sharp mental image of our face. If we run our fingers over our face, we can sharpen this mental image and give ourself a complete facial massage. Once the image is crystal clear in our mind, the massage is complete.

1 With your index fingers, trace the outline of your face: begin at the centre of your forehead and move your hands downward and away from each other. Bring them together at your chin. Do this three times.

2 Using your index fingers again, trace circles around your eye sockets. Do this ten times.

3 Now place both hands on your face so that your little fingers meet at the tip of your nose. Smooth both hands over the contours of your face, gently stretching the skin as you move your hands away from one another, giving you a sense of the plains and hollows in your face. Do this five times.

4 Smile softly to accentuate the creases of your cheeks between your nose and the corners of your mouth. Trace out these creases, top to bottom, with your index fingers. Then, when you reach your mouth, follow the line of your top lip. Now trace out the shape of your smile by moving your fingers over your whole mouth. Your mental picture should be complete.

The Flow of *Qi*

*I*ncreasingly, the West is looking to Eastern philosophies and therapies to complement, expand and counterbalance its own traditional views. In the Chinese book of wisdom, the *Dao de Jing* (6th or 5th century BC), the author Lao Zi describes how everything is made from nothing. From nothing came yin and yang, interdependent opposites. The energy that flows between yin and yang is known as *qi* (alternatively spelt *ki* or *chi*). In Chinese and Japanese medicine, *qi* is believed to flow through all things, both animate and inanimate.

Q*i* is thought to pass through twelve main channels or meridians in the body. Each channel is associated with a different bodily organ, and along each are points that may be accessed or stimulated to treat physical and mental disorders caused by blockages to *qi*. When *qi* flows easily through our bodies, we feel relaxed. But when *qi* becomes blocked (for example, by negative thoughts or self-doubt), its flow is hampered and this may cause stress, ill-health, arguments and accidents. Two of the main meridians are those of yin and yang. If *qi* is blocked in either of these channels, we have a yin and yang imbalance — believed to be a main cause of stress.

Although many people remain sceptical about unconventional medicine, we should remember that Eastern methods have been successfully practised for centuries. Finding a local practitioner is the best way fully to benefit from the natural therapies of the East, as he or she will be able to talk you through the process of harmonizing with your body's energy. However, the Japanese therapy *shiatsu* ("finger pressure"), a massage technique in which static pressure is exerted along the meridians of *qi* to free the energy flow, can be practised alone or with a partner: listed opposite are the basic methods.

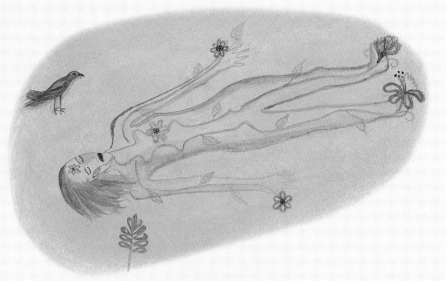

Shiatsu for Stress

Connection *shiatsu can deal with shallow breathing and shortness of breath caused by stress. Lie on your back on the floor and ask a partner to place the palm of one hand on your abdomen and of the other on your breastplate. Hold still for one minute. The flow of* qi *between your lungs (breath) and kidneys (the "seat" of anxiety) will be made easier, helping you to breathe more deeply.*

Dispersal *shiatsu can be used to free the energy flow in the neck and shoulders, where the physical tension of stress often occurs. Lie on your front and ask your partner to disperse the blockages in your neck and shoulders by rocking (pushing the flesh forward and back while pressing down), circling (moving the balls of the hands in a circular motion over the flesh while pressing down), squeezing (gripping and letting go) or stretching (moving the hands in opposite directions as they pull and press down on the flesh) the muscles in this area.*

Finger pressure *shiatsu to the centre of the right palm, and just below the ball of each foot, will calm the mind and emotions. Ask your partner to exert gentle pressure on these points in turn, as you lie comfortably. This will aid the flow of* qi *to your mind, sending the energy coursing through your body, and leaving you in a peaceful state of relaxation.*

The Self and Relationships

Our first and most valuable relationship is with ourselves. Unless we are comfortable in this union, we are unlikely to feel comfortable in any other. Yet so often we avoid meeting ourselves by living on the surface of our lives, doing rather than being, and never making time for introspection.

Relationships form the greater part of our preoccupations. Our parents and siblings, our friends, our husband or wife, and then our own children, are the other characters in the drama that is our life. We interact with them on every level, yet only after we have discovered the inner self can those interactions bring all the rewards that potentially they offer.

Whenever we send out an emotion or a signal, its message is sent back to us. The French Existentialist writer Jean-Paul Sartre said, "Hell is other people." But this is only true when "hell" is the message that we transmit. If our own inner world is in chaos, a turbulent mass of anxieties, fears and emotional baggage, it is very easy to blame our stress on others: as we project it, so it comes back to us, like a far-flung boomerang. Only by sending out positive signals from ourselves can we be free from the negative emotions of others. In this way we may restore relaxation within ourselves — feeling good inside and good about the people around us.

Personal Identity

Our deepest fear is not that we are inadequate. Our deepest fear is that we are powerful beyond measure.

Nelson
Mandela
(1994)

*F*rom the first time that, as babies, we recognize ourselves in the mirror, we learn to base our sense of identity on our outer appearance. If someone asks us to describe ourselves, we give our name, the colour of our hair, our height and shape, and then perhaps our occupation, our marital and economic status, our religion, and so on. But is this really who we are? For most of us there is only a very small chance that a stranger could truly know us by the labels we have given ourselves.

If probed further, we might go on to describe ourselves by our feelings or circumstances: "I am a sad person," "I am unlucky." This approach, however, is just as inaccurate: we may feel sad, and we may have been the subject of misfortune, but these facts are not what we are. We cannot *be* our emotions or our circumstances, because these aspects are transitory.

Identifying with our labels gives us a sense of personal security. We feel comfortable with the descriptions that we give ourselves because they provide us with identity without our having to face the deeper aspects of self. However, the idea that our labels (the boundary posts of our comfort zone) represent safety is a myth. By fencing ourselves in, we run the risk of another person pulling up a post or two by perceiving us dif-

ferently from the way in which we perceive ourselves. The gap in the fence undermines our self-confidence because it goes against what we have taught ourselves to believe. Even if the label challenged is a "bad" one, such as "I am unattractive," our confusion may prevent us from deriving positive value out of the other's esteem.

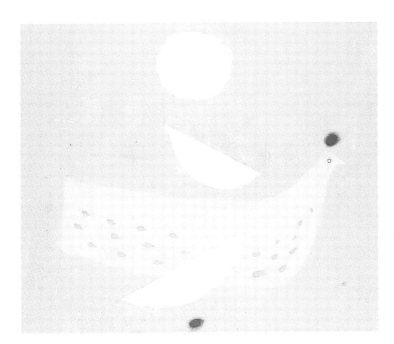

*Not to be cheered
by praise,
Not to be grieved
by blame,
But to know
thoroughly one's
own virtues
or powers
Are the
characteristics of
excellence.*

Saskya Pandita
(1182–1252)

Identity can be easily confused with the roles that we play (parent, boss, and so on). As a result, we might find ourselves playing the wrong role in a certain scene. If our role as a professional becomes our identity, we might, while at home, behave as if we were in the office. This can lead to friction as we interact: our partner may dislike being treated with the distance that we should reserve for our colleagues. Matching our thinking with the scene we are in means learning that our roles are merely the leaves of a tree whose roots are our true self.

Awareness of the differences between our roles and our true identity (and of the influence of our roles on our actions) also helps us to cultivate an understanding of others. If someone does something wrong, or something against us, we are able to see that they too may be acting from an inappropriate sense of self. They have momentarily lost the plot. This insightful understanding is the basis of compassion, enabling us to reach out with more relaxed and forgiving hands.

Personal Mythologies

*W*hen we are children, our developing picture of self is determined by what we hear about ourselves: "What a beautiful girl," or "He is very shy." The culture of home is the foundation of our self-image. Our parents' and friends' comments about us form the first labels that we give ourselves, and help to provide the basis for our outlook and behaviour.

As a result, we each have an internal committee of voices. Whenever we want to try something new or difficult, we subliminally recall the legacy of opinions: "Don't do that, you might hurt yourself," "I wouldn't try anything so ambitious," and so on. Such simple statements fashion our expectations of ourselves, and can make us fear the consequences of action.

We not only listen to such voices, we also embellish them. We create myths about ourselves that explain our behaviour. A parental comment such as "He's very shy" can become "My parents favoured my brother and neglected me, so I have always been very shy." Or, "She finds it very hard to make friends" becomes "I can't form relationships because my parents always quarrelled." We use our mythologies to gain sympathy and affection; as reasons to opt out of projects that we find daunting; and to explain our failures. But our anthology of mythical excuses serves only to perpetuate self-doubt.

To be totally honest about ourselves, avoiding the temptation to mythologize, is difficult, but it is the only route to self-understanding. Self-knowledge lies deep within, at our "centre". Meditation is one route there (see pp.122–5), stilling the mind to let us focus on our inner needs and unabridged thoughts. Visualization exercises, such as the one opposite, can also help free the mind of illusion and encourage clear insights into positive aspects of the self.

A Voyage to the Centre of the Self

Exercise 13

Personal understanding lies far beneath the surface of the self, a great distance from the clamouring voices of labels and personal mythologies. We might call this place our "centre", the true core of who we are. This visualization will help you to locate your own place of truth.

1 Sit comfortably in a quiet room. Close your eyes and breathe deeply for a few moments. Concentrate on stilling your mind.

2 Imagine that you are floating in a warm ocean. Sunlight falls on your shoulders. You drift without effort.

3 Now you are gently swimming beneath the ocean surface, feeling increasingly calmed by the water's caresses. Just beneath you, the wreck of a galleon is visible. This is the outer shell of your psyche.

4 As you approach, you see that the ship's woodwork has rotted. You swim in through an opening. The further into the galleon you swim, the cleaner and brighter the water becomes.

5 At the centre of the ship, unspoilt, lies a chest of precious objects, each one an aspect of your true self. Spend time re-discovering yourself. Pick up each object and reflect on its meaning. A coin might represent your honesty, a chalice your generosity. Swim back to the surface, relaxed in the knowledge of your worth.

The Power to Change

*T*o a greater or lesser extent, we have been given power by a number of influences — parental, educational, cultural. Over time these influences have also shaped our habits of thought and belief. Power is energy with a purpose, but anything that has become habitual has lost its purpose, and so forfeited its power. The power to change is essential if we are ever to annihilate stress, which is crucial if we are to relax.

In her book *Feel the Fear and Do It Anyway*, Dr Susan Jeffers encapsulates the result of habituation: "If you always do what you've always done, you will always get what you've always got." In other words, unless we break habits and re-focus ourselves to change, we will always feel unrelaxed because we will never be able to break patterns of negative thinking.

We all have vast reserves of energy inside ourselves, but when purpose is lost and self-expression is blocked we fail to tap these phenomenal resources. The danger is that we will start to live on the surface of our lives, no longer active, but reactive. Unless we find and use the power to change, we drift at the mercy of random currents.

We cannot rely upon anyone else to do the changing for us. Self-belief and self-empowerment come, by definition, from within. When we undertake to change, we are the heroes of our own spiritual journey. And, like the great heroes of myth, we must slay the demons of illusion (low self-esteem, laziness, attachment to habit) with the sword of knowledge and the shield of courage. It may help us to dramatize our resolution in these terms. Devise a programme for change, as an idea; persuade yourself that the idea can be made real; then pour your energies into carrying out the project. This is how dragons may be brought low.

The Alphabet of Change

Awareness *First, become aware of what you need to change in yourself. What is preventing you from attaining contentment? What habits are blocking the way to realizing your full potential? What do you want to be in the future? What is your vision?*

Belief *Many people entertain change in their minds as a kind of fantasy. But in fact it is a reality that lies within your power. The belief that you cannot really alter your life will not stand up to challenge. It might be useful to ask yourself questions such as "What has held me back from change in the past?" and "What are the stages by which I can bring change about?"*

Commitment *Motivation is the key to commitment. We need to want to change, rather than feel it as a duty to ourselves. Try writing down a list of commitments in the form of statements beginning with "I will". They should come directly out of, and be connected with, your overall vision. Personal power is released with every promise to yourself that you fulfil.*

Discipline *We cannot change unless we are able to maintain a steady course over time. Think of each sign of change as a major landmark passed. Even if we find ourselves slipping into old habits, that achievement cannot be taken away. We do not have to cover the same ground again: every time we step forward we are covering new road.*

The Paradox of Purpose

Our "life purpose" is the overarching journey that gives some kind of shape to life. We might say that we seek simply "happiness" — although the term really means nothing until we understand how happiness manifests itself for us. Or we might set out to feel closer to nature. After defining our purpose, the next step is to identify the changes that will bring it to fruition (letting go of material attachments; moving to a rural community). These are our goals. To achieve them we set objectives (giving up certain luxuries; learning skills that we can use to gain rural employment).

With regard to finding relaxation, what matters is that the trajectory of our life purpose provides a shelter in which we can genuinely find calm. There is a pattern to our life, and however accurately the pieces come together, we know at least that we are not merely drifting. We can relax without feeling that we are neglecting the inner self.

To be content in the shelter of our purpose, we must feel that it is capable of being turned into reality. In other words, we must overcome fear of failure. If we become too "attached" to the goal, we maximize our chance to fail. The paradox is that in order to serve our vision we must specify our goals and objectives, but we must also be prepared to *let go* of these targets. This is not a sign of feeble mindedness or lack of commitment: rather, it is a sign of wisdom. Leting go of our goals or objectives, we become more relaxed in our attitude toward them. The journey ceases to be burdensome and stressful because we don't have to strive: life will present us with the right opportunities, and we would be wise to have faith in this prospect. Our life, in any case, is a trajectory, not an imperative. We can retain our integrity even as we modify our aims.

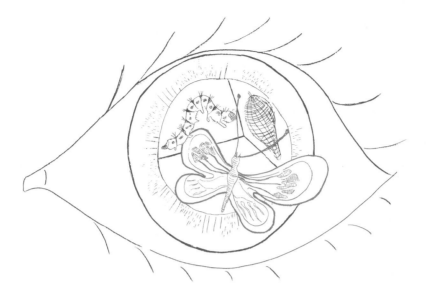

The Rules of Attraction

If we are alert to opportunities that will satisfy our most serious vision in life, it is surprising how often those opportunities will tend to present themselves. These are the rules of attraction — the almost mystical ways by which a need and its fulfilment are drawn together.

Create your vision. *Think about how you see yourself in the future. At this point, your purpose may be intangible — you might want to become a wise or more caring person.*

Identify your goals, objectives and tasks. *This is a matter of expressing your general direction in more concrete terms. Your goal might be to understand Chinese wisdom; your objectives to learn the principles of Daoism, Buddhism and Confucianism by a certain time. Your tasks might be to find a teacher of these subjects and, say, to read the* Dao de Jing.

Make yourself a magnet. *This means having faith that you will encounter the relevant opportunities and recognize the signs they are giving you — which may not be direct. Look out for such signs with patience, and act on them when they come.*

Making Peace with Your World

*T*he idea of peace can be as mystical as we wish it to be. At one level, peace is simply the removal of aggression and threat, both inside and outside the self. At a deeper level, it is a total declaration of the heart, an acceptance of the otherness of others, the stilling of all inward protest — our own modest blessing on an imperfect world.

At the opposite end of the ethical spectrum lies blame, and the belief that if we let blame attach itself to us, it will stigmatize us, and damage the ways in which others see us. Where tensions are to be resolved, the solution is seldom to take the blame entirely, because this is still to live in terms of blame. We must learn to dissolve blame, to declare an emotional amnesty by which we banish our own residue of aggression or grievance, but still retain responsibility for our own actions. If we are able to neutralize these negative emotions by invoking a state of peace, an imbalance within ourselves is corrected.

Peace, in the public realm, is ceremoniously declared, and in the personal realm too there is much to be said for enacting a ritual of intention. Formalities help us to impose personal sense on the flow of mental and emotional states. To some degree declaring peace is what the philosopher J. L. Austin called a "performative" statement — not purely descriptive, but an action in itself. This can be as true of the inner world as of the outer. However, the formal declaration is valuable only if we prepare for it by ridding ourselves of negative feelings, and vow (again, note the formality) that peace will be permanent.

Emotional Amnesty: a 3-stage Declaration

Make a list of ten people or situations that are undermining your ability to relax by provoking negative emotions. Using the following procedure, attend to these one at a time, perhaps devoting a few evenings to each one. However, do not spend too long trying to sift the rights and wrongs: remember, most situations have a shared cause.

Set aside time *in the evening. Relax in a chair, eyes closed. Empty your mind; let go of your preoccupations one by one. Imagine a pitch-black night. Think of this interlude as a watershed in your life, an empty pause between phases.*

Summarize the essence *of the problem to yourself. Conjure up the issue in visual form if possible. Resolve that you are going to be able to contemplate this image in future without emotion.*

Declare peace *with the situation. It is no longer a grievance or source of anxiety. Imagine a jagged blip on a screen being levelled to a continuous line.*

The Art of Kindness

*T*he seventeenth-century French courtier Larochefoucauld wrote that often our virtues are merely vices in disguise. Altruism can make us feel good about ourselves, but self-admiration is far from admirable. Kindness is a composite quality, in which love, understanding, foresight, empathy and selflessness can all mingle, but in order to be true this virtue must be free from ulterior motive – including self-esteem. Yet so long as we give to others in a thoroughly outgoing, uncalculating frame of mind, there is no doubt of the blessings that we derive. A simple act of kindness, pulsing along the web of connections bind-

ing us to the world, can regenerate positive feelings that spread in all directions.

The Eastern principle of *karma* teaches that every word and action are seeds that grow to bear the fruit of an appropriate result. The seed is not the initial act, but the thought that procures that act. So, if the thought (the seed) is morally wholesome, selfless and genuine, we have better karma and will be re-born, after death, into a happier, more spiritual life. If the thought is unwholesome, selfish or untrue, our karma depreciates, and our next incarnation will be less favourable. Whether or not we hold with reincarnation, the philosophy remains true across cultures: as we sow, so we shall reap; kindness reflects back smilingly at the giver.

Placing other people's desires before our own can be difficult, especially when we feel that we are "losing" something in the process. We should always remember that by treating kindly a person who may have been unkind to us, we can break ourselves free from the damaging cycle of blame. Selflessness is not denial but affirmation, not servitude but leadership.

Day-to-day Karma

Meditate, *once a week, on the virtues of someone you know. Begin with someone you like, then try the same exercise with someone for whom you have negative feelings. The next time you see these people, try to recall all the good things that you found in them.*

Make a positive gesture *of kindness in an unexpected encounter. If you bump into someone you know in the street, offer to help them carry their shopping, or buy them a coffee so that you can talk for a while. Don't let time be your jailer.*

Offer gifts *spontaneously. The next time you go on vacation, buy lots of small presents without having specific people in mind. Carry a few around with you to give them away on a whim.*

Prepare kindness *if you have a meeting planned with someone whom you have never met before. Give them a gesture of appreciation for the time they have set aside for you. For example, you might arrive at a meeting carrying refreshments.*

The Search of the Heart

Although in theory our passage from the relationships of childhood to those of adulthood should be
seamless, in practice this can be one of the most stressful transitions of our lives. Often protected from loneliness as children, we are conditioned to believe that finding
a partner and having a family are the norms in life. So, in ado-
lescence or adulthood, we strive for these "goals", hurt ourselves
for them, and fear loneliness to such an extent that we often
remove ourselves far from the rewards of both solitude and,
self-defeatingly, of love. By trying too hard, we fail to achieve
the desired vision.

*Happiness is the
absence of striving
for happiness.*

Chuang-tzu
(*c*.350BC)

Solitary pleasures are often those most keenly felt. Unless
we can relax alone, for days at a time, we are missing a special
experience that we should all be able to enjoy regardless of
whether or not we are in a relationship. We might be seeking
a partner in life, but it is philosophically and spiritually
unsound to accept that this unfinished quest should be a cause
for anxiety: we must trust in the future, and concentrate in the
meantime on pursuing our own interests, allowing our personalities to grow. Anxiety about our prospects of finding
love, or for that matter friendship, will almost inevitably
erode our chances of success.

In the typical Hollywood movie, the most attractive character (regardless of looks) is frequently the least needy, the one
who finds love *because* he or she has not expected it or connived
at it. This idea may be accurately projected into
real life: a self-contained personality, calm and
purposeful, is the most powerful magnet.

Imagine that your inner self is a flower. In
order to protect your flower from the hurt that

Love is infallible;
it has no errors for
all errors are the
want of love.

Andrew Bonar
Law
(1858–1923)

you may once have known, you place it inside a steel case. Starved of light, water and nutrients, and locked up unwittingly with all the negative emotions of past experience, your flower soon loses its appeal. If you can set free that negativity, by an effort of self-belief based on self-knowledge, your flower will blossom again in the sunlight. Before long, it will be rich in colour, with a captivating fragrance, each petal soft to touch. The beauty of the inner self, similarly, will radiate through your smile, your eyes, your mannerisms, in countless captivating ways. If there is no peace in solitude, there can never be peace in love.

The Relationship Adventure

*L*ove is often envisaged as the original state, before our loss of innocence. We might imagine love in Paradise as pure and platonic, a rapport between two souls uncompromised by sensual desire. But in reality, when love begins to strike, many of us fall to pieces, becoming almost incapable of sensible behaviour. The term "lovesickness", though colloquial, in fact has physiological foundation. When we "fall in love", our adrenaline levels increase so that our breathing becomes shallower, our heart beats faster, our palms become sweaty, and our nervous traits become more animated. We might say that "lovesickness" is the stress of being in love.

Arguably, the enemy of love is not hate but fear. Having found someone with whom we might want to share our lives, we panic. Suddenly we feel vulnerable, conscious of who we are and of the signals that we are transmitting to our new-found partner. We are acutely aware of what we have to lose, and so make conscious efforts not to stumble in our precarious journey toward mutual fulfilment.

One result is that we begin a series of games. Afraid of appearing too enthusiastic, we might vow not to call the other person, but to wait for them to call us; we might try to be enigmatic about our plans for the weekend; and so on. At the same time, our hopes might be mingled with fears. We might imagine that we must change, to become the person whom we think that our partner desires. And we might fear that our identity or our freedom will be undermined. In this way we become embroiled in various deceits and contradictions, which confuse both ourselves and our potential partner, and are counterproductive.

The key to making our way through this difficult part of our adventure is to go back and rediscover the confidence that we once had in ourselves. If we can muster some emotional intelligence, by rationalizing and expressing how we feel (not necessarily to our potential partner, but perhaps in a diary), then we can more easily keep the complications of feeling under control. Bear in mind that we are still ourselves. We are not yet a "couple", simply an affinity biding its time.

To relax with our new relationship, we have to understand that the journey of mutual discovery requires honesty — with ourselves and with the partner. If we believe that we need to change to make the partnership work, there is little to be gained from short-term, strategic change: better to confront the real difficulties and devise a long-term programme for the relationship that is sustainable without compromising your true self.

The Established Bond

Relationships are inherently complicated. Creating a balance of power so that two independent personalities may live in harmony can at times seem impossible. The established bond requires a continual process of adaptation and renewal, and with both of these there is potential for some degree of stress.

The blurring of boundaries between gender roles in modern society means that the terms of relationships are more open to negotiation. Work, domestic responsibilities and children may well be priority items on the agenda.

In order to sustain an established relationship, we need to understand what each expects of the other and what we expect for ourselves. We must express ourselves honestly; avoid initiating guilt or blame; and be forthcoming about our insecurities (while at the same time being prepared to look inside ourselves to try to resolve them from within).

Relationships can deteriorate silently, as minor grievances fester into resentments and tenderness falls by the wayside. Eventually such pressures can explode into full-scale confrontation. Keeping channels of communication open is paramount if the bond is to remain strong and fulfilling.

Banishing stress in the established bond demands that we give each other both time together and time apart; that we guard against blame or jealousy; that we laugh together even during periods when we face serious issues; and that we take opportunities to express tenderness in thought, word and deed. Think of the bedroom not as a testing-place for the relationship (this is disastrous), but as a sanctuary for both parties, a place where truces are delared and love restored.

Cultivating Empathy

This exercise will highlight which of your uncertainties you have communicated to your partner effectively in the past, and which you have held inside. Likewise for your partner. Use your discoveries as a basis for an open discussion about the direction that your relationship is taking.

1 Sit with your partner in a quiet room. Don't sit opposite one another, which would be too formal, but in a position where you can retain reassuring physical contact – perhaps on a sofa. You should both feel as relaxed as possible.

2 Sit silently for a few minutes, each trying to see yourself as your partner sees you. Start by visualizing how you appear physically to them, then think about the impression you make in your behaviour, your speech, your daily routines.

3 Playing the role of your partner, talk about the concerns you have about your relationship. In other words, you are telling your partner what your impression is of what he or she is thinking – especially with regard to doubts and insecurities. Then allow your partner a turn at role-playing in a similar way.

4 Regain your true identities. Talk calmly and honestly through the things you have each said, sifting their accuracy. Pinpoint any omissions or misperceptions.

Relaxing into Passion

Surely passion, with its connotations of turbulence and compulsion, is far from relaxing? But if we build a wall against passion, relaxation is impossible. Scientists have demonstrated that if the *amygdala* (the biological "seat" of passion) is removed from the brain, we lose our ability to function on *any* emotional level, preferring to be solitary than to interact. We become indifferent to the people for whom we once felt love, and uninterested in the activities that once inspired us.

Of course, there are occasions when passion can be as blinding as anger, preventing us from seeing clearly and behaving rationally. The violence that sometimes erupts at political rallies shows how dangerous passion can be. On the other hand, commitment to a set of beliefs, or to a person, can be extremely uplifting. Finding "our passion in life" awakens a slumbering potential, making us feel vital and renewed. We are then ready to project a refreshed sense of purpose into other, unrelated, areas of our lives. From passion we gain our enthusiasm for life as a whole.

We tend to think of passion in terms of the physical aspects of a particular relationship. However, physical desire is the offspring of physical attraction, and our outward appearance changes over time. Although we may not lose our physical attractiveness as we age, we do lose our resemblance to the body, skin, hair, mouth and so on with which our partner was first enamoured. Relationships based solely on the physical will seldom stand the test of time. Spiritual passion, however, transcends physicality and allows us to feel unconditional love, not just for one other person, but firstly for ourselves and then for *all* aspects of our life.

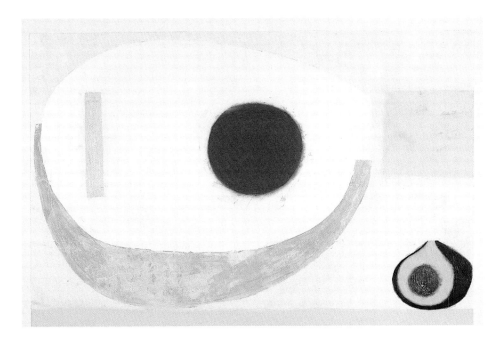

Ultimately, for succesful relationships with ourselves and with others, we need to be sure that we have passion clearly defined as a *spiritual* seat of the self, not a physical one. Understood in this sense, passion injects us with enthusiasm for life.

Enthusiasm is not without its dangers. Left to its own devices it can carry us along at a reckless pace. When passion veers out of control we experience desire, a highly unrelaxing force. Once desire begins to overwhelm us, our sense of true passion is lost. To pull ourselves back on course, we can apply the brake of reason – intelligence deployed to correct the instincts of the heart. We might also think of the brake as moderation. Aristotle swore by the doctrine of the Golden Mean, a belief in steering the middle course. Passion, understood as giving rather than consuming, is a virtue, not an instinct. Think of a river channelled between the beautiful banks of a city. The flow is unimpeded. The river augments, rather than spoils, the graceful urban masterpiece.

I count him braver who overcomes his desires than him who conquers his enemies; for the hardest victory is over the self.

Aristotle
(354–322 BC)

95

Sex in Perspective

As we look at the society in which we live, we see all around us an obsession with the body and with sex. The covers of dozens of magazines remind us of this fact each time we walk into our local bookstore. Like any other form of obsession, sex can bring anxieties into relationships.

At the outset, we concern ourselves with how long we should wait before consummation, and whether both parties are willing. Once this hurdle has been overcome, we have the additional pressure of past physical relationships, and, therefore, comparative and competitive performance. In an established bond, the sex obsession may take the form of keeping alive physical attraction, because our social mindset is such that if we don't have good sex in a long-term pairing, we believe there is a fundamental problem. In fact, this need never be the case.

Putting sex in perspective means stepping back and viewing human relationships, and love, in terms of four levels of union. Sex, the *meeting of bodies*, represents the physical and lowest of the four levels. In essence, sex is not synonymous with love, and emotional fulfilment through love is readily attainable without intercourse.

The next level is the emotional one: the *meeting of hearts*. This is a magical experience, when we know that we have the same feelings, at least for the moment, as the other person. Then we have the *meeting of minds*, when both partners think the same way, or one says something that the other was already thinking. This is a special demonstration of love. Conversations take place without a word being spoken, often through a knowing glance.

But the highest level of love is the *meeting of spirits*. In this state we walk with ease through each other's worlds without fear or barrier. Trust and acceptance are total – a situation that is rare

in relationships, but one that we may need to rediscover if ever we are to attain complete relaxation within our union. If a letter arrives for our partner, we have no nagging impulse to read it to check for unacceptable intimacies. If a stranger of the opposite sex calls, it does not even occur to us that something illicit might be going on.

Whenever sex begins to cause problems (for example, on account of performance anxieties), it is worth bearing in mind that its value is secondary to that of love. Abstention from sex, at least for a mutually agreed period of time, can often restore the fundamental stability of the relationship. At the same time, it is a classic technique for revitalizing a physical life — in the same way that fields are left to lie fallow in order that they might replenish their wholesomeness.

A Theory of Relativity

If family minds love one another, the home will be a beautiful flower garden.

The Buddha
(568–488 BC)

*W*e tend to grow up amid tensions of various kinds – even in the happiest homes. This is unsurprising, given that the family unit is one of the few places in life where we are able to express ourselves openly and honestly. Our family is made up of the people who have seen every "face" we might show and the aftermath of every emotion we might feel. The decorums that so often shield us from conflict in other walks of life – formality, politeness, modesty – are pulled down by sheer force of intimacy within the family, so that we stand exposed to uncensored, sometimes turbulent emotion. At the same time, however, the love of family is the closest that many of us will ever come to unconditional love. Hence, we gain hope and strength from the domestic sphere.

It is in families that we learn the principles of relationships. No two families are the same, but psychologists have shown that "healthy" families need not be havens of peace. To show anger or frustration is better for us than keeping those feelings locked in. If a taboo is placed on displays of anger, the child who cannot help expressing such emotions feels guilty for doing so. Conversely, unexpressed anger makes him or her feel out of control, isolated and fearful – a response that some of us carry into adulthood. Clearing the air of our grievances in an environment of mutual support and understanding, where there is no fear of lost love, can be liberating.

However, the danger in this is that we become so "involved" with the emotions of our family that we suffer from excessive dependency. Siblings, or parents and their children, may so often look to one another for help that they forget how to help themselves. Furthermore, we may feel such close empathy that

*The family
is like a fortress at
the top of a hill —
it is built to
weather even the
most violent of
storms.*

if, say, our sister feels sad, then we take on her sadness; and, rather than helping constructively, we become sad too. By establishing clear levels of independence from one another, we are more able to offer genuine support and advice.

When serious family tensions break out, we may similarly absorb the headaches into our own lives — even when the problem centres upon a relationship over which we have little control. This is a common cause of stress. An example would be an adult becoming anguished about quarrels, under a different roof, between his or her parents. As a close relative, there might be very useful steps that we could take to mediate between the two protagonists. But we should bear in mind that independence sometimes means leaving others to sort out their own differences.

Families work best when everyone agrees that there are some issues that fall outside family jurisdiction. A network of support works better when it is not at the same time a web of amplified anxiety.

Growing into Childhood

*I*n the course of our lives we pass through not one, but a number of childhoods: our own, our children's, our grand-children's, and, if we are lucky, our great-grandchildren's. Our own childhoods are partly determined by those of our parents. The culture of parenting filters down through the generations, slowly adapting and changing, but usually with a recognizable inheritance.

However, children come to terms in various ways with the rules to which their parents expect them to adhere, and often there is tension between the two sides. This may be because the parents are learning from the wrong model. If, as parents, we try to step into our own parents' shoes, recalling what they tried to teach us, we may perpetuate an outmoded template. Instead, greater insight might come from actively trying to re-experience our own childhoods, remembering how it felt to be on the receiving end of parental care.

Recall of the child's-eye view gives us an immediate advantage. We begin to remember what made a deep impression, what made us happy, what made us frustrated. As you watch your children negotiate life's surprises, try to put yourself imaginatively in their position. Trace in detail the profile of their day — you might even write an imaginary diary from their viewpoint. For parents to share in the innocent adventures of childhood, rather than seeing parenthood in terms of con-taining chaos and restoring order, is fulfilling. From our chil-dren we can re-learn how to experience the world's marvels. Their senses are alert, their memories unclouded by repres-sion, their imaginations unfettered by habit. As we travel around with our offspring, we might think of them as gurus, instructing us in fresh ways of perception.

Psychologists believe that babies and toddlers bond much more quickly with older children and adolescents than they do with adults. As grown-ups we strangle the child within us because in an adult world the direct, uncompromising perceptions of childhood are, in many ways, regarded as irresponsible or unsophisticated. Yet to experience life directly, as a child does, is a basic prerequisite of relaxation.

As adults we tend to like people who like us, to be susceptible to flattery, to be anxious about what we say and how we appear, to be reluctant to play, to find it difficult to express enthusiasm or emotion. Layers of habit, like interior scales, have accumulated upon the child within ourselves. Part of the art of relaxation consists of prizing off the scales that separate us from a true perception of the world and a true relationship with others. If we spend time with children, and pick up from them how to unlearn the worst habits of adulthood, this process of purification may become much easier.

Fearless Encounters

Nobody is emotionally independent. We all inhabit a landscape whose contours are aligned to the personalities, moods, expectations and demands of other people. Most of us tend to vary in our behaviour according to the people we are with. With certain people we feel confident, able to express ourselves to the full; with others we may be uncertain, reserved, or simply unable to make a connection. This inconsistency does not make us characterless or schizophrenic: rather, it is a function of our ability to see how we appear from another person's perspective.

Combining a true sense of self with the intuition we need to show understanding toward others is part of the adjustment to the world that we learn as we grow up. But in some of our encounters as adults we are inevitably going to have to negotiate such adjustments afresh — for example, when we feel overshadowed by someone we perceive as especially gifted, intelligent, or otherwise "superior". And in situations where we are being judged (as distinct from merely imagining that we are) — in an interview, or when addressing a gathering — the stresses that we feel can be even greater.

Our discomfort probably results from our own insecurities projected on to the image that we believe the other person holds of us. Where this is the case, we must bring about a shift of perspective. By an effort of imagination, we can visualize alternative views, as in the exercise opposite. Once we accept that we are less disadvantaged than we feel, our confidence grows and our performance improves, in a virtuous spiral of increasing self-esteem.

Spotlight on the Self

Exercise 15

A state of relaxed alertness will yield optimum results in an interview. To relax, you need to defuse all sense of confrontation, instead seeing the meeting as a friendly factfinding exchange and an opportunity to talk quietly of your achievements. Your skills are being sought, and the questions asked of you will be designed to elicit their precise nature. You have only to answer them truthfully and articulately to present yourself to good advantage.

1 Think of your interviewer as someone with whom, very soon, you might find that you have a great deal in common — perhaps not a friend, but someone you enjoy talking to.

2 If the interviewer seems very formal, this is because (s)he is doing his job the way he believes it should be done. Imagine that he is nervous and concentrate on putting him at ease.

3 If the interviewer seems unfriendly, say to yourself: it is because he or she has difficulty with the situation. Respond calmly and pleasantly.

4 Imagine the interviewer doing something else: jogging in the park, or cooking dinner, or riding a horse.

5 If the questions become difficult, think of a friend who is spectrally in the room — perhaps standing behind the interviewer. Imagine this friend urging you on, applauding your handling of the situation, willing you to succeed.

Calm Assertion

*W*e can all remember times – probably more often than most of us would like to admit – when we have walked away from a encounter chastising ourselves for not saying what we meant to say. We may even have had time to rehearse our "pitch" and yet still failed to come away with our goals achieved.

Being tongue-tied and feeling guilty about our agenda are tell-tale signs of a chronic lack of assertiveness. We are not necessarily undemanding people: it is just that we find it difficult to articulate calmly what we should like to say. The result is usually increased anger and frustration. Within a relationship we might vent this anger on our partner, thus closing their ears to our demands and damaging the prospects of harmony still further. At work, where we are required to act with decorum, we more often turn the anger inward and feel increasingly dissatisfied with our job, even to the point of resigning.

On the other hand, most of us have also experienced the positive feelings of freedom, relief and relaxation that come after we have put our point across and at least reached a compromise on our desired outcome.

Self-worth is the foundation stone of assertive behaviour. Without believing that we are worthy of improved terms, in any aspect of our life, we will never be able to assert our needs convincingly: our arguments will fail to cohere and we are more likely to back down, or to nod in agreement when we mean to say no. The key is preparation: if we fix in our minds, before the encounter, the essential points that we will unwaveringly state, then whichever way the debate goes we shall at least have made clear our point of view.

Effectiveness depends, also, on being sure that another's actions can help us to achieve the needs that we have so

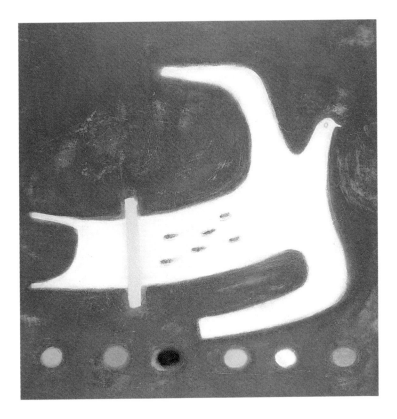

concretely defined. It helps to understand, in advance, the other's viewpoint, because this way we can anticipate any barriers that might legitimately prevent the other person from wholeheartedly yielding to our wishes. Yet, having made this excursion into the other's realm, we must not pitch camp there: the exercise is to present our own case, not automatically to concede the validity of the opposing view.

There are times when others will try to manipulate us into believing that our requests are unreasonable. A common ploy might be attack or criticism on an issue that is tangential to the main agenda. Anyone unsure of their ground is likely to try diversionary tactics. To present our case successfully, we must patiently wait for the best opportunity to bring the discussion back to the centre. Sometimes, repetition is necessary: never feel awkward about reiterating a point as a way to bring the dialogue back on course, or simply for emphasis. It is more effective to re-state an issue quietly than to express it more loudly or more vehemently. Concentrate on remaining calm, and confidence will follow; and with confidence, you are likely to make good progress toward a workable resolution.

Within a close relationship our emotions tend to be much more keenly felt, and it will be harder to keep a check on ourselves. We might be tempted to open old wounds, or misuse our intimate knowledge of the other person for rhetorical effect. The main thing to remember is that to talk about our emotions is not necessarily to re-experience them: in telling our story, it helps to remain distanced from the feelings that we are describing. If allowed to re-awaken at full strength, our emotions can sabotage articulate presentation.

Our waking lives are in large measure dedicated to our relationships and our work, and our contentment within these areas radiates outward, to anyone who comes into contact with us. For fulfilment in these spheres (and the relaxation that this brings) calm assertion will often be needed. The sequence opposite sets out the main points to consider before asserting a point of view.

We cannot expect people to "read our minds" or to guess at our discomfort — however well they know us. We are only fully known by what we say, though our continual inner dialogue with ourselves often makes us forget this. Expressing how we feel and what we are looking for without being shrill, confrontational or unrelaxed is a basic skill that may be called upon at any time, in any situation. It is worth cultivating.

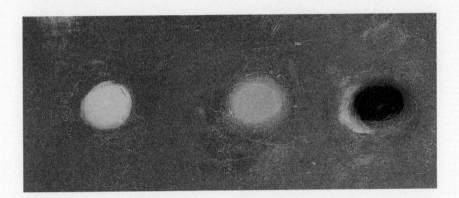

Making Yourself Heard

Identify your goals. What are your needs? To what degree are you prepared to compromise? What is your acceptable middle ground? How long are you prepared to wait for a result?

Rehearse your argument logically. Why do you deserve these goals? What are the logical steps toward them? You might like to visualize these steps as milestones along a road. What preparation must you make before you can embark upon your journey? In what ways are you unable to proceed without the cooperation of others?

Empathize with the other person. Consider how your requests might be difficult for them. What objections might they throw in your path? How can you propose ways around these difficulties and bring the conversation calmly back to your objective?

Avoid attack or criticism of any other person, and yet never undermine yourself. Always keep the discussion focused on you — your circumstances, what you feel, and what you want. Don't, for example, be tempted into blaming another colleague or friend for your dissatisfaction.

Breathe slowly and evenly so that your voice sounds steady, calm and confident. You may also benefit from doing a breathing exercise before your conversation to help calm any nerves and focus your attention.

Crying and Catharsis

*I*n our post-psychoanalytic age, crying is socially sanctioned as therapeutic. The implication of the phrase "burst into tears" is that there is a release in crying, that we set free pent-up emotion and feel more relaxed after doing so. There might indeed be a feeling of relief that finally we have expressed our instinctive responses. Physiologically, however, crying causes shortness of breath (sobbing is the body's desperate attempt to replenish oxygen levels) and tense muscles, neither of which benefit long-term relaxation.

If we believe that crying is an antidote for stress, we are in danger of tricking ourselves into thinking that, once the tears have stopped, the problem that upset us has been at least partially resolved. This is not necessarily the case. The tears may have been triggered by deep-seated factors that still lurk below the surface, though the outlook for a while seems calm again.

Seeing someone cry tends to make us panic: we fumble to stop the tears as quickly as possible, imagining that once the crying has ceased, so will the pain. This is rather like imagining that switching off a fire alarm will douse the conflagration.

If tears have been triggered by an argument, an illusory truce will often follow. A complex chemistry of sadness, guilt and sympathy brings about reconciliation. Hugs and apologies are freely given. Fatigue may also play a part in blunting the edge of the quarrel. Yet the underlying causes remain, and may soon flare up again with increased vehemence.

Unconsciously, we may become so used to gaining attention by bursting into tears (we learn this when very young) that every now and then we play a few rounds of the "crying game" – particularly in the context of a relationship. If our partner is upset, we may

even resort to crying as a pseudo-proof that we are more hurt than they are. In this way, crying becomes part of a strategy — an emotional manipulation, which serves only to heighten tension, and let peace slip further from our grasp.

As an immediate form of pain-relief, crying *is* cathartic. But we must never forget that the release afforded is temporary: one day we will need to find alternative resources. To do this, it is necessary to avoid being a seasoned traveller in the vale of tears. Crying is a sign of hurt, and hurt, revisited too often, can start to feel comfortable. Its familiarity engenders trust: the terrain is *reliable*. To leave the land of hurt may require a decisive step in a different direction, to the world where others are making the best of their lives. This is the land of potential contentment. That does not mean that, to begin with, we can *fulfil* our potential here. But the first step after major sorrow is deciding that this is where we will take up residence, in the hope of becoming naturalized.

Laughter and Absurdity

*H*earty laughter stimulates beneficial, even life-preserving, chemicals in the body. The short-term effects are dramatic: tension is dispersed, apprehension is banished, our ability to think positively is increased, and contentment is restored.

Children will readily laugh at themselves, but adults are wary that self-mockery might be seen to undermine our commitment to "grown up" responsibility. In fact, being unable to laugh at ourselves may indicate that we find it hard to recognize our own foibles. We then become susceptible to pomposity, pride, vanity and the like.

Life, like comedy, can be absurd and unpredictable, and events can take unexpected, even unwelcome, turns. If we lose the plot, forget our lines or become drawn into the action in ways that are unanticipated, the loss of control should not necessarily be lamented. All we need do is change our perspective to see the absurdity of our predicament and laugh at it.

The importance of the comic is that it punctures our pretensions, allowing an inrush of fresh air into consciousness. It is thus a relaxation technique *par excellence*. Often, we will laugh *despite ourselves* — in other words, the comic spirit wholesomely breaks down inner barriers, working against the force of gravity (the pun is intended), undermining our resistance to delight. The consequent sense of release is palpable.

In an age of impromptu wit, the well-rehearsed joke, moving from premise to punchline, is perhaps becoming a dinosaur. Yet the genre should not be undervalued. Jokes, like myths, serve a purpose in society. To tell one, especially to a group, is to assume an important mantle — that of storyteller. Breaking down inhibitions, uniting an audience in a shared, involuntary response, the joke-teller is an agent of relaxation.

Caricaturing the Self

Comedy revolves around the bizarre and the unpredictable, and is thus a way of negotiating circumstances that might from some viewpoints seem threatening. By laughing at our powerlessness, at the ways in which events conspire to question the dominance of our will, we can accept and even enjoy our predicament. Laughter is a corrective that prevents us from becoming complacent in our control over our environment.

Comic moments can form an entire repertoire of anecdotes. Drawing upon these, we can cheer ourselves by amusing others. Think about the absent-minded things you have done recently. Perhaps you were chopping mushrooms while waiting for a jug of coffee to filter and then, when the coffee was ready and in a cup, "poured" mushrooms into it instead of milk?

Comic characteristics are largely the things that are "typical" of us — a facial expression or reaction that friends might say represent us. These might form the basis of jovial, exaggerated self-mocking: "You know me, I always scream if he refuses to do the dishes!" Such observations lighten the burden of our "being" by enabling us to laugh at (and, importantly, with) ourselves.

Having Faith

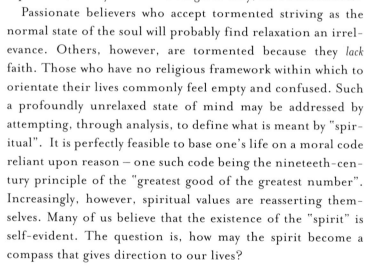

Since the dawn of history most people have believed that life is unsustainable without faith. For some, secure in the knowledge of God's love and a blissful afterlife, religious belief has provided a cushion of contentment. Elsewhere faith has brought anguish. Conflicts between soul and flesh, belief and experience, family bonds and religious duty, have scarred lives.

Faith is the state of being ultimately concerned.

Paul Tillich
(1886–1965)

Passionate believers who accept tormented striving as the normal state of the soul will probably find relaxation an irrelevance. Others, however, are tormented because they *lack* faith. Those who have no religious framework within which to orientate their lives commonly feel empty and confused. Such a profoundly unrelaxed state of mind may be addressed by attempting, through analysis, to define what is meant by "spiritual". It is perfectly feasible to base one's life on a moral code reliant upon reason – one such code being the nineteeth-century principle of the "greatest good of the greatest number". Increasingly, however, spiritual values are reasserting themselves. Many of us believe that the existence of the "spirit" is self-evident. The question is, how may the spirit become a compass that gives direction to our lives?

As a starting point for self-analysis, consider whether the following statements are evidence of the reality of the spirit. We respond to beauty. We believe that the self has a non-material essence. We believe that certain spiritual teachers (such as the Buddha and Christ) had profound understanding. Dreams give us glimpses of a non-material reality. We have an innate sense of good and evil. Music can awaken important feelings. The world is extraordinary. If we can agree with these points, we might be closer to faith than we imagine.

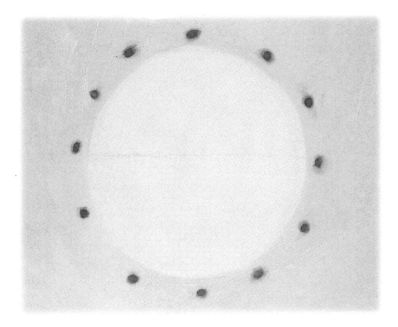

If you have faith as a grain of mustard seed, you may say to a mountain, "Move to this other place;" and the mountain will move.

New Testament (Matthew 17:20)

A Letter from the Spirit

Many people who recognize the importance of the spirit have difficulty in envisaging the form that the spirit might take. Material analogies capture spiritual truths only imperfectly. But perhaps the best way to understand the spirit is as an intelligence that can change your life if only you listen carefully to its voice and heed its message.

Imagine that you have a spiritual parent — call him or her God if you wish. Or, if you prefer to avoid labelling in this way, imagine that he or she is simply the voice of your spirit or soul. If this "parent" were to write you a letter, what would it say? In what ways would your parent's love for you be expressed? What would be his or her hopes for and expectations of you? Remember that he or she sees only the best in you. Find a quiet spot, where you will be undisturbed, and write the letter that this spiritual parent would send to you. Keep it in a safe place and read it whenever you feel your faith in the spirit is being undermined.

Varieties of Counsel

$\mathcal{W}$e all feel in need of advice from time to time. Sharing our concerns with another sometimes seems the only way to analyze our situation and decide on the way forward.

There are numerous therapy options available to us. One of the most effective is co-counselling. This puts us in touch with a person unknown to us, to whom we explain how we feel, while also allowing them to unburden themselves to us. Such two-way sharing can establish an illuminating dialogue – even if the other person's stresses are different from our own. We may find it easier to relax and be open with someone who is not otherwise involved in our life. Professional counsellors also have this aspect to recommend them, as well as their wealth of training and experience.

If we are to benefit from counselling, we should never expect to be presented with answers. Self-understanding comes from within, and anyone else's advice can be expected only to guide us on the route to self-knowledge so that we may find our own solutions.

With this in mind, we might conclude that the best counsellor, after all, is our own self. Strangely, when we look to others for guidance, it is often because we need validation for the advice of our own inner voice. Whenever we seek reassurance in this way, we run the risk that our advisor's counsel will differ from our own, sowing seeds of confusion in our minds. If, instead, we can learn to formulate and heed our own advice, we may be able to navigate our way through life's dilemmas with more assurance. One approach is to dramatize, through creative visualization, that part of the self in which we have most faith – the inner counsellor who penetrates even our most self-deceptive strategies.

Counsel with the Self

Clarify *the apparent (surface) reasons for your unease. What symptom or symptoms caused you to notice how stressed you are? What recent events may have triggered this tension? Each time you identify a stress trigger, ask yourself if a deeper trigger lies beneath it.*

Separate *your immediate symptoms of unease from the very deepest concerns that underlie them. Try to find quick solutions for the symptoms — you might use creative visualization to imagine them flying out of the window. Then prepare to tackle the more fundamental issues.*

Counsel *yourself by closing your eyes and imagining yourself as an* **alter ego** *sitting opposite you in a chair. What questions does your other self ask you? What are the most honest answers to those questions? Do you trust the counsel of your alter ego? If so, open your eyes and set about heeding your own advice — it is the best you will ever hear!*

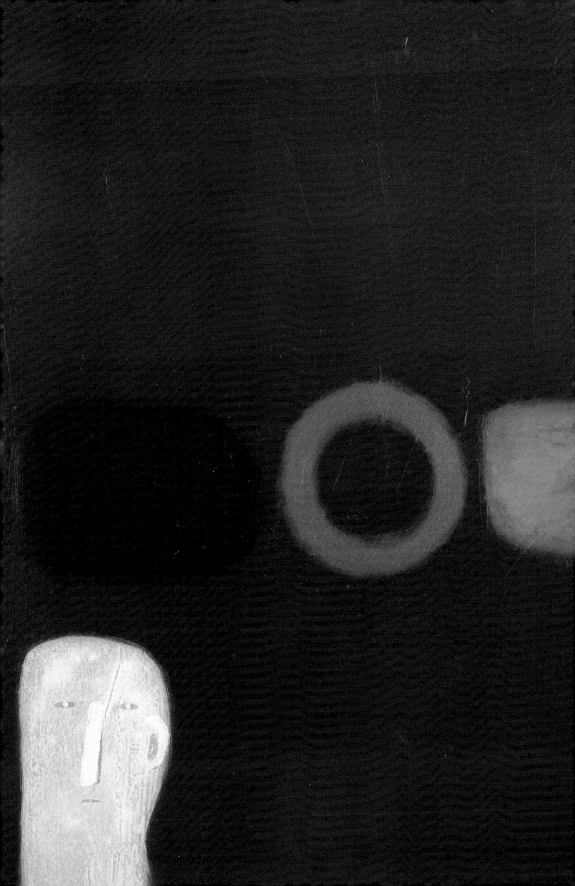

Mind Power

*T*he mind is the seat of all our beliefs, perceptions, experiences, memories and aspirations. It is the most powerful machine we have at our disposal, and also the one whose controls are most difficult to work.

Learning to use the power of mind for self-exploration will help us to root out the causes of some of our greatest anxieties. It will also enable us to discover some vital aspects of ourselves that lie buried beneath the collected habits of time. We might imagine that our mind is like an acorn, glued to the end of a long piece of string. As we progress through life, the acorn rolls over the string, which gradually winds around and around the seed, so that the ball created grows bigger and bigger. Eventually, the acorn, the essence of who we are, is buried so deep that it is lost altogether. Finding relaxation through "mind power" may involve gradually unwinding the ball of string until finally we rediscover important truths.

Meditation is one of the most powerful techniques of the mind. Through this age-old discipline, we can rid ourselves of the distractions that have come to dominate our perceptions and responses, and can re-connect with the pure, still, radiant centre of the self. We can also harness the power of our dreams and of our senses (the corridors between inner and outer worlds) to help us rediscover within ourselves a deep sense of calm with which most of us have lost touch.

Silence and Noise

Our towns and cities are loud with the sounds of perpetual endeavour, the car has moved from being servant to tyrant, and people rush from errand to errand with less time than ever to give each other. Increasingly, we feel an urge to escape these pressures that assail us. In reaction, we recognize an emotional call that pulls us back toward simplicity. At the heart of this feeling is a power much more elemental than anything that industry or city life have to offer — the simple, healing power of silence.

Expressing a profound aspect of creation, with overtones of infinity, grandeur and the sublime, silence should never be regarded as merely nothingness or emptiness. A composer knows that the silences between notes are as much a part of composition as the notes themselves. We can apply this analogy to our own minds. If we are thoroughly self-aware and monitor our thoughts for a few moments, we can become conscious of the spaces between and behind each new passage of thinking. This is our inner silence. Meditation is as much about attending to, and in the process prolonging, this silence as it is about purging our thoughts of impurities.

Noise can be stressful if we cannot allow it to surround us without experiencing the frustration of desperately wishing that the noise would stop. Silence can be stressful when we are addicted to our distractions, and afraid of confronting the inner self stripped bare of the reassuring props of habit. Yet in silence there is deep balm for the spirit; and properly attuned to its positive qualities, we can almost feel it washing over us in a motion of pure grace. When sound and silence are in perfect alliance, as in the rhythmic wash of surf on a beach, we enjoy a rare fusion of matter and spirit that everyone should savour whenever they have the chance: head for the ocean, close your eyes, and open yourself up to harmony.

The Random Concert

Exercise 16

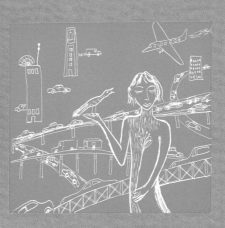

Uncontrollable noise can be a major irritant, and leads to tensions, even fights, between neighbours. The following exercise is designed to place extraneous noises in a less anxious perspective, by defusing them of their threat to peace, and accentuating their positive aspects.

1 Do this exercise in your garden or backyard, or on your porch. Or sit in a park near a busy street, or on a street bench. (You could also adapt the exercise as a creative visualization.)

2 Sit comfortably. Drop your shoulders and breathe deeply. Close your eyes and spend a few minutes concentrating on any sounds. Begin with the nearest, then move out.

3 Once you feel that you can hear everything possible, focus your attention on one sound near by.

Choose one that is pleasant to listen to, and also clear. Perhaps you can hear a bird chirping, children playing, or distant music?

4 Move on to other sounds. Try to perceive them as part of a pattern. The road-menders, the traffic sounds, are all part of a vast modern symphony, and you are privileged to share the peformance. Imagine the good things that the sounds evoke — the ambulance rushing to someone's aid, the construction of a new hotel with fine views over the park.

Relaxing with Time

*W*hy, as the end of a vacation approaches, or even after the half-way point, do we often feel that the quality of our leisure time becomes subtly compromised? Why do we value so much, at the beginning of a weekend break, the sense of time stored up — an account on which no debits have yet been drawn? The answer to these questions is simple: we have not yet learned to accept time as the medium that enables us to relax, rather than as the obstacle that prevents us. If we can succeed in thinking of time not as a precious, slowly depleting commodity that has to be filled with exciting episodes to make life worthwhile, but as the vehicle of fulfilment, just as the body is the vehicle of the spirit, then we will have taken an important step in working toward harmony and balance in our lives.

Increasingly, our lives are ruled by the clock, but clock time is a human invention made to serve us. We must not allow the measurement of time to dominate our thinking, or we will sabotage ourselves in a self-fulfilling cycle of anxiety undermining success. Can we break this cycle, once we are trapped in it? Certainly we can, if we train ourselves to come to a more philosophical understanding of the nature of time, refuse to let clock time feed on our minds like an incubus of anxiety, and live more fully within the moment by tuning our inner self more accurately to the world outside.

The first step is to break down our sense of linear time as a relentless succession of milestones. In order to counteract this reductive view, it helps if we try to attune ourselves more sensitively to our body-clock, and at the same time reinforce our

Psychological time and scientific time travel in the same direction — but in another universe this might not be so.

Time is nature's way of preventing everything from happening at once.

The distinction between past, present and future is only an illusion, albeit a stubborn one.

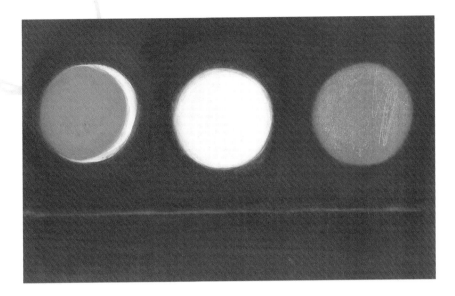

understanding of natural cycles — the seasons, the phases of the moon, the migration of birds. Family life is necessarily clock-bound, but try to find periods in your life when you can hide your watch and gear your actions to your natural inclinations — having a meal when you are hungry, going to bed when you are tired. Cooperating with our own body clock is a prerequisite for true relaxation.

The future, though seemingly empty, may in fact be richer than the richest parts of the past.

The Paradoxes of Time

If we think too much about time, we will tie ourselves in philosophical knots — and distract ourselves from the goal of relaxation. Yet to meditate occasionally upon some of the many paradoxes of time can help us to ensure that we are not too much enslaved by the tyranny of the clock. In the margins here are some statements intended as food for thought, inspired by various bodies of belief, from Eastern mystical texts to the theories of the New Physics. Reflect on the paradoxical nature of time, but without trying to *solve* the paradoxes: they are not puzzles, but mysterious truths.

If we try to entrap a fleeting experience, we destroy it: the way to wholeness is to kiss the moment as it flies.

Living Patterns

*T*he "comfort zones" of life are defined in large measure by our habits. Although they may grow initially out of our deepest needs, eventually our habits can harden into a barrier all around us that prevents us from realizing our full potential. If habit is comfort, and comfort is relaxing, then what is wrong with enjoyable routines — a weekly walk around the park, an annual vacation to the same hotel, with family or the same friends? The answer is, nothing — so long as the habitual pattern that you develop is not deadening your responses to the rich stimuli in and around you. The problem is that the more habitually we do something, the more our experience of it tends to become stale, and the more lethargic we become about finding new stimuli.

Habits of thought create unrelaxing habits of behaviour. If we look back over a typical day, we will often see that it conforms to a familiar pattern. We expect that it will take us half an hour to be fully alert in the morning, so it takes us half an hour; we expect that we will feel frustrated by the first interruption to the day (because it breaks our routine), so we feel frustrated. We fear so greatly any upset to our "usual" living patterns that we fixate on fortifying our comfort zone against the unexpected. Living in a comfort zone is like being a bird freed from its cage only to fly around a small room: there is no real freedom.

We fear spontaneity because it is unreliable. However, by jumping over the fence of our comfort zone, we can fully experience life, and thus learn and grow. Every moment is an opportunity to splatter our linear patterns of thought and behaviour with flamboyance and colour. Each minute of habit is a minute of spiritual inertia; each minute of freedom is a minute of relaxed wakefulness.

Breaking the Hold of Routine

Recognize your routines. Map out your week. What spaces do you have when you cease to be governed by responsibility to work or family? What are the habits that fill those spaces? What experiments can you do to see how you might change these habits?

Question the living patterns of your week. How much of your time is spent mundanely because you are too lazy to do something different? Are you learning from each day? Does each day hold any moments of special significance, such as keeping a promise to yourself or to another?

Prioritize the things that fulfil you most. Do you have any unrealized hopes or promises? These may be simple things, like finding time to visit an old friend. Build them into the pattern.

Wake up to your real needs, and fashion new living patterns around them — more flexible patterns that readily adapt to new circumstances and new interests.

Inner Space

*T*here is nothing mysterious or difficult about meditation. Many people believe that they would be unable to practise the art, because it would require the dedication and spirituality of an Eastern ascetic. Anything that we perceive as difficult may, of course, *turn out* to be difficult, in a self-fulfilling prophecy. But meditation is really a sophisticated version of something that many of us do quite naturally from time to time – that is, become lost in thought. If we applied ourselves to the discipline, we could undoubtedly become as spiritually effective as a Buddhist monk. However, we can achieve beneficial levels of relaxation without going that far.

Like a desktop, the mind can become strewn with so much information and detritus that we are unable to find our way to the bottom of the disorder and so function effectively. We clutter our minds with experiences, worries, regrets, negative self-images, memories, actions, reactions, emotions, analyses, hopes and fears – all in a protean stream of consciousness. Every time we do or say anything, or have anything done or said to us, we add another distraction, and our true self gets buried deeper and deeper.

Meditation is intended not to stop us thinking altogether (this really would be extremely difficult, if not altogether impossible), but to help us to order the confusion. Through meditation we can begin to focus upon constructive thoughts, and start to discover positive images and ideas of ourselves. When we become lost in thought, we tend to daydream about a better future; or we might reflect on a problem in order to prompt a range of possible solutions. Meditation aims to do the same things, but in a more purposeful way: it maintains its

In order to find Perfect Wisdom, one must go through the door and see one's self-nature.

Ancient
Chinese
patriarch
(7th century AD)

focus on the subject, whereas a daydream might wander off along a random tangent. By relaxing our minds through meditation, we can clear our desks and experience a renewed sense of self. This will bring with it identity, clarity and freedom, in a cascade of revelationary thinking.

Knowing who we really are is at the heart of our potential for contentment. If that sense of our identity is based on other people's opinions, or on the pressures that others place upon us, then our self-esteem runs out of our control, rising or falling at the will or whim of others, like a thread of mercury in a thermometer.

The soul who meditates on the Self is content to serve the Self and rests satisfied within the Self.

Bhagavad Ghita
(c.400BC)

Meditation can gently steer us away from this emotional dependency to put us back in charge of our own lives. By helping to restore a true relationship with ourselves, it gives us a firm footing on which to establish strong and equitable relationships with other people.

Such is our addiction to action, we may find ourselves saying that we don't have time for inward reflection – or that it is self-indulgent. We feel that we will lose our dignified sense of purpose if we are not constantly *doing* – helping, building, improving, moving forward. However, these are precisely the circumstances when our real needs become obscured – blurred by our own momentum. Time spent organizing our inner self is time gained for clarity and fulfilment.

Many of us hardly spend a single minute thinking about ourselves – or if we do, our thoughts may tend to be selfishly calculating. Meditation is unselfish, as its aims are to better, or purify, ourselves so that we may live happier, healthier lives, which impact upon all those around us.

As a first step toward meditation, practise the exercise opposite – a basic visualization, in which the mind imagines a vivid inward journey. Words or syllables may be used in meditation (a mantra may be chanted to still the mind), but there are definite benefits in using visual techniques, which may more readily solve the problem of what the mind should do if it is not to flit randomly over our preoccupations.

Meditation has been practised for thousands of years in Eastern cultures. It has taken different forms, but its essence remains the same – to find inner peace so that our adventures in the world are calm, contented and purposeful.

A Five-step Meditation

Exercise 17

A first step in meditation is to be able to introspect without fear or compromise. This exercise takes you through an open door into the vast labyrinth of your unconscious so that you may begin to appreciate and love who you are. Sit comfortably in a pleasant room and close your eyes. (You may like to recite the exercise onto a tape so that you don't have to remember it.)

1 **Withdraw** energy mentally from everything around you — not to reject or resist, but to turn your attention inward. You might think of how a tortoise withdraws into its shell to detach itself from the outside world, but carrying the experience of the world with it inside its shelter.

2 **Create** a point of consciousness. Focus on the centre of your forehead. Think of this point as a radiant star. This will transmit positive energy, making you feel good about yourself.

3 **Affirm** this positive energy through positive thoughts and images about yourself, such as "I am a conscious being," or "I am a peaceful soul."

4 **Focus** your energy on peace, and let this become the object of your meditation. As you focus, you will give peace life, turning a thought into a feeling.

5 **Experience** this feeling by "watering" it with your full attention. This is the beginning of self-realization through meditation.

Outer Meditation

*M*editation enables us to achieve self-awareness and self-realization (a true sense of who we really are), with the ultimate aim of helping us to change. The first and most basic type of meditation helps us discover a positive sense of identity (see p.127). The second type moves away from meditating on a single point inside our heads to meditating on an external object that holds some symbolic reference for us.

In Eastern doctrine, meditators use *mandala* and *yantra* designs for external meditation. These are highly decorative, complicated, symmetrical images, charged with religious symbolism. The meditator "connects" with the symbols and uses them as reflections of traits in his or her own personality. In this way he or she gains a deeper insight into the inner self.

We can begin more simply by finding in nature something (real or imagined) that holds particular symbolism for us. The symbol can be anything, so long as its associations are positive – we might choose a lake, a mountain, a river or a tree.

Whatever we find in this symbol will have correspondences within ourselves. For example, by meditating on a flower, perceiving and focusing on its various attributes, we can awaken our awareness and enhance our experience of our own spiritual attributes. The form of the flower's many petals may be seen to correspond to our virtues; the fragrance may correspond to the vibrational quality of our thoughts; and the colour may allude to some of our positive moods or emotions (green for our love of the world, red for calm assertion, blue for enveloping sympathy). What we see, in the moment of meditation, is what we are – as we appear without, so we are within.

Focus on a Flower

Exercise 18

Nature is a virtue in itself: what could be more beautiful, more calming? Through meditation on a natural feature (illustrated, real or imagined), we connect with such beauty in a way that reinforces, by reflection, our own qualities. A real flower can reveal the flower of the spirit.

1 Use the image above (or a real flower) as a basis for meditation. It is shown here in one colour – how do you bring it to life? What attributes do you give it so that it seems more perfect for you?

2 Concentrate on this completed image. You should be completely focused on the flower, and no other thoughts should enter your mind.

3 What symbolic resonances does the image have for you? How might these qualities reflect aspects of your self?

4 Now consider each different attribute you have given the flower. Contemplate each in terms of how it might correspond to your personality.

5 If the flower has any negative aspects (is one of the petals drying out?), what might this be telling you about yourself? Concentrate on mending the negative, making your self-image wholly positive.

6 Connect with the object in this way, until you feel that the beauties you see are a direct reflection of your virtues.

Positive Transactions

*P*erhaps the greatest challenge in learning to relax is to sustain the art of tranquillity through the various interactions of the day. Practising techniques of relaxation in our free time is all very well, but we will never progress toward increased calm if, each time we return to our mundane responsibilities, we wind ourselves up again into a state of high tension. The secret is to carry through, into our active lives, all the lessons that we have learned through private relaxation.

Our attention tends to focus on the signals that others transmit to us. So, if someone at work appears to be criticizing a certain plan, we automatically reflect that negative feeling back at them. Criticism breeds blame and ill-feeling. If we can think more positively about our transactions with others, and look for the best in what someone is saying, and in their personality, we can begin to transmit positive energy toward them, and thus defuse any potentially unrelaxing situation.

This may sound idealistic, but is not as difficult to achieve as we might think. Just about every utterance or action that we hear or see can be understood to have a foundation of positive intent. The woman who complains that a colleague isn't up to the job is keen that her organization functions efficiently. The man who insists that other children are less intelligent than his own is a devoted father. Looked at in this way, negative and positive are co-existent, like yin and yang. If we focus our consciousness on the positive, we arrive at a more holistic view of our relationships with other people.

We might also improve our transactions with ourselves and with our own work through "complete effort". This involves concentration on our various activities, one at a time, being careful to complete each task as fully as possible.

Complete Effort

So numerous are the tasks that we try to get done each day that we rarely get the chance to do things completely — we might read only half a chapter of a book, having meant to read the whole chapter; or clean only the upstairs of the house; or cut a business meeting short. "Complete effort" encourages us to try to focus our minds on only one thing at a time. We concentrate on it so deeply that we do not become distracted until it is completely finished. We will find that other people are far less likely to interrupt if we seem completely focused on our task than if we appear to be rushing around juggling many things at once. Fewer tasks may be *started* each day, but there is ample reward in the knowledge that anything we do start, we will finish. This frees us from the frustration and anxiety of leaving things half-done.

Mindfulness

*W*e all know that our minds are power centres — the crucible for all thoughts, ideas, imaginings, decisions. They are also the instruments by which we are able to concentrate — and deep concentration, as we know if we have meditated, is a valuable route to relaxation.

Central to Buddhist philosophy is the concept of the Middle Way. This encorporates the Eightfold Path, the route to enlightenment, at the end of which is spirituality. One of these paths is mindfulness, the ability to hone concentration to become completely absorbed in a particular task or object.

In daily life, we tend to make automatic judgments about phenomena. We assume, for example, that there is nothing grand or powerful about a grain of rice. However, fundamental to mindfulness is the concept that no such judgments are made and no emotions are felt about the object or action in which we have become absorbed. We simply harness the power that is concentrated when our mind becomes focused on a single action or object instead of being scattered in thought. Thus, we can reach inner peace by finding value in the smallest, seemingly most insignificant things. In the words of the Buddha, "What is little becomes much."

Mindfulness helps us stop or slow down. If we become mindful of digging in the garden, we cease to make the activity strenuous by trying to get it done quickly so that we can get on with something we perceive to be more relaxing. Instead, we become fully absorbed in the action. We will not feel compelled to complain about the exertion, because we will not judge the task, and so we will not feel tired. In fact, we will actually find strength in the power of the action.

The Five Powers of a Focused Mind

The power of perception *allows us see into things and truly understand them, with neither complication nor confusion.*

The power of choice *requires us to distinguish right from wrong, and good from bad. Having done so, we can select our option, and at every moment choose to be positive.*

The power of inner energy *can spur us onto new things, encourages us to change where we feel uncomfortable with ourselves and help us to enjoy life to the full.*

The power of injection *can permit us to energize others with our own positivity. As we help them to feel positive, good energy bounces back toward us to perpetuate the positive cycle.*

The power of mindfulness, *by which we absorb ourselves into any action or thought without distraction or complication, further energizes us by allowing the power of our mind to become concentrated, freeing us from ties of frustration, anger and petty-mindedness.*

Dream Lives

Our dreams reflect the preoccupations that beset us in our waking lives. We may wake from a bad dream feeling troubled for a few minutes, and then dismiss the experience as a curiosity. But in fact the dream could be pointing to some deep anxiety – perhaps an unresolved memory from childhood, an unacknowledged desire, a problem of self-esteem. If we recognize that dreaming is the method by which the unconscious communicates its insightful wisdom to us, then we can benefit from dreams as cues for improved self-understanding in waking life. With their help we can face up to our hidden tensions, then negotiate these tensions and put an end to needless anxiety. Once we have reached this level of self-awareness, we will find that our dream life becomes less troubled. This is the point at which we can finally begin to use dreams positively, as aids to relaxation.

The language of dreams, based upon symbolism, is notoriously cryptic. If we find a relationship claustrophobic, this might be expressed as trying to do handstands in a room with a low ceiling. If we are troubled by criticism at work, this may be symbolized as being arrested for driving too small a car down the highway. The main point about dream interpretation is that the attempt itself will usually open out useful perspectives on the self. There is no way to confirm the validity of dream symbolism: the unconscious runs no helpline. But if, in a spirit of courageous truth-seeking, we start to explore possible meanings for the symbols, there is no doubt that we will arrive at constructive insights. In time, these insights are likely to settle the dreaming mind: with self-understanding comes a more relaxed attitude to life, and with this comes more restful sleep.

One of the most profound varieties of relaxation occurs after the kind of dream that leaves us feeling happy and fulfilled. At such times the unconscious itself is relaxed. We might doze awhile, savouring the dream that has reflected our most valuable hopes for the future, our happiest memories, or the truest qualities of our closest friends or relatives. Waking, we will feel rejuvenated, with energy in abundance.

Some people are able to cue good dreams by meditating on their desired subject — perhaps a favourite landscape, or a cherished friend, or spiritual fulfilment — for a few minutes before they go to bed. An image fresh in our minds as we drift to sleep might well be carried into the unconscious. Although success is not assured, this cuing method can also be used experimentally as a first-aid technique to counteract troubled dream-content.

Re-awakening the Senses

*m*odern living can be a hazardous business. We spend our time worrying about past or future, or else busying ourselves with distractions, urgent asides, frantic travel. Either way, we lose touch with something vital to our sense of well-being: the connection between ourselves and the world around us, conducted through a precious gift that we all take for granted — sensation. By re-awakening our senses, and using them to strengthen our contact with the world, we can counteract the separation that many of us feel from the life around us.

Our five senses are the essence of experience. It would be a mistake to relegate them to the role of the body's navigators, safely steering us through the rough-and-tumble of phenomena, while the mind concentrates on more elevated matters. Parallelling the sense of emotional self, which we gain from all our thoughts, memories and feelings, is the "biological self" inherited through a genetic transaction at the head of many centuries of evolution. Our five senses remind us of our physical side. If we can recover for them some of the importance they once had for our distant ancestors, we can begin to restore lost aspects of ourselves, so that mind and body are brought into better equilibrium. And at the same time, we can enjoy more fully the rich adventures of our environment.

By re-awakening the senses, we learn how to slow down. We focus more narrowly on the present, and our mind moves in a natural, linear sequence from one thing to another: first the lightning, then the thunder, then the first drops of rain on our hands and faces. This is the joy of registering with our senses the pace of events as they happen. By concentrating on the world of sense-impressions, we can take a well-earned vacation from the mind's routine concerns.

The Cat in a World of its Own

Exercise 19

When we stroke a cat, it purrs with the pleasure of touch. Its acute hearing enables it to distinguish between the sound of its owner's footsteps and those of other people. Its heightened sense of smell can tell it when its owner has been with other cats. And its keen eyesight enables it to pick out detail in the dark. The exercise below will help you to rediscover the simple satisfactions of sensory perception — just like a cat.

I Curl up in a ball like a sleeping cat, on some cushions on the floor. Close your eyes and breathe deeply.

2 Become aware of how heavy you feel; concentrate hard on your weight pressing into the cushions; be comforted by them supporting you.

3 Open your ears. Listen for any sounds. Pick each out individually and put them together as a whole.

4 Slowly open your eyes. Concentrate on and appreciate each thing you see as it comes into focus.

5 Push yourself over onto your knees, which remain tucked underneath your chest. Stretch out your arms and rock your torso forward so that you are on all fours. Arch your back toward the floor and then toward the ceiling. Now sit up. Spend a few moments absorbing everything around you.

The Senses in Balance

Our five senses are windows onto the world through which energy flows in two directions. The senses receive impressions from the world, and at the same time transmit our personalities to others. They are also closely bound up with emotional experience and with communication. Our eyes receive a constant stream of visual messages, but we may also use the eyes to show how we feel. Through our ears we hear the sounds of life; while by "lending an ear" we give comfort to others. In our mouths we can taste an unlimited variety of flavours; but through the same orifice we convey our best jokes and wisest counsel. Touch allows us to experience texture; but can also transmit love and reassurance. Our senses are not merely instruments, but deep-rooted aspects of the self.

In order to lead a balanced life, we must try to keep our sensory experiences in harmony. So rich is the pleasure of the external that there is a danger of dependency. We cannot live good lives on pure sensation. If we define ourselves in physical terms, we begin to think that happiness depends on something "coming in" rather than something "going out". The truth, however, is that goodness and contentment, themselves closely interdependent, are aspects of the self that we transmit. To give is the greatest blessing, and the highest use of the senses is to express the self in the most generous way possible.

Eastern thinking brilliantly depicts the government of the senses in the image of the body as a chariot. The self is the charioteer; the five senses are the five horses. The self keeps the senses harmoniously working together, curbing their tendency to bolt out of control. They work in the service of a higher purpose. The journey would be impossible without them, but equally impossible if they were allowed free rein.

Narrowing Sensation

Exercise 20

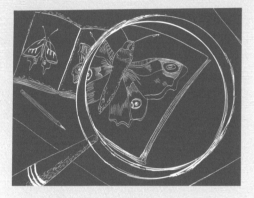

One reason we may find it difficult to relax is that the world comes rushing through all our senses without discrimination. Because of this, we feel that we are out of control, and the experience can be as harmful to us as falling asleep to our senses altogether. The exercise here helps us to be more selective in the sense impressions that we allow in, and guides us on using them once arrived.

1 Once you have read through this exercise, imagine that you are a tiny Tom Thumb-like figure sitting inside your head, just behind your eyes. Look out through the windows of the eyes at this book, as if it lies in the hands of another person.

2 Study the exact size, colour and shape of the book. Be aware of the edges, corners, thickness, and so on – all from the perspective of a miniature self. Study the book in such detail that you are aware of nothing else.

3 After a few moments of complete absorption, look up and find another object in the room to approach in the same way. Be careful not to make any value judgments – just see the object as it is in this moment.

4 Practise this exercise twice a day, and adapt it to work for other senses (you might blindfold yourself and encounter an object through touch). Being able to control your senses, and concentrate more powerfully, goes hand in hand with the ability to relax.

Freeing Thought

Perhaps the only place where we can truly be free is in our minds. However, thought is susceptible to the growth of restrictive routines. Often, our anxieties become habitual, and in thinking through possible solutions we fall back on the same responses. Trying to get to the heart of a maze over and over again, we fail each time to learn anything from the wrong turnings taken. Freeing thought from habit is one of the most difficult challenges we face in our quest for fulfilment. Any attempt to do so immediately hits an obstacle: the fact that thought is both the object and the medium of our analysis. It is easy to become entangled with paradox, with the result that we feel a knot of frustration tighten in the mind. If this happens, stop thinking, and do something physical and routine. The aim is to cut through, rather than add to, layers of complication.

When trying to bring order to the potentially chaotic landscape of the mind, it helps to identify four levels of thinking.

Levels of Thought

The first (lowest) level is *negative thought*. This is critical, angry, fearful, egotistical and lazy; it will breed only sadness and unease. The next level is *wasteful thought*, in which we tend to brood over the past. We worry about what has or might have been, and spend time feeling anxious about the things that we can't control. Then we have *necessary thought*, such as "I must buy food," and "I must pick up my child from school." The highest level, though, is *positive thought*. This breeds peace, love and creativity, and encourages harmony and happiness. By becoming aware of these levels we can free our thoughts through choosing to elevate them to the highest level, thus liberating them from the shackles of habituation.

Aspiring to the Sun

Exercise 21

The sun is an appropriate image for positive thinking.
This visualization uses a sunlit landscape as an analogy for the four levels of
thought described opposite. Use it to increase your percentage of positive
thoughts every day.

1 Envisage a beautiful valley with a lake, forested foothills and high mountains rising up into the clouds. This is the landscape of your mind.

2 Your position in this landscape and the form in which you are manifested depends upon the quality of your thoughts. Are you a fish swimming in the murky depths of the lake (negative thoughts)? A frog jumping back and forth from the shore to the lake (wasteful thoughts)? A human, wandering into the forest to gather food and build a shelter (necessary thoughts)? Or the sun, which sustains all life on earth (positive thoughts)?

3 Now think over all the thoughts that you have had through the day. How many of these can you attribute to a particular level? Make a promise to yourself that each day you will try to increase your quota of positive thoughts and banish negative and wasteful thoughts from your mind.

Relaxing with the Elements

𝒲hen we are tense we often feel "drained" physically and emotionally: our mouths become dry, our bodies feel fragile, and we say that our nerves are "brittle". Only when we relax and express our emotions do we regain a more fluid state. Sometimes we might even "dissolve into tears", or "melt with desire". These metaphors of fluidity are not arbitrary. They arise from the close affinity between our physical and mental states, and water. If we are rested and at peace, our actions and feelings tend not to occur disjointedly, but as a harmonious flow. The endless dance of water (a universal symbol of life) can be thought of as analogous with a healthy, happy state of being.

Ancient yogic texts advise meditation near waterfalls, rivers and lakes. Carl Jung spoke for many in his description of lake scenery: "The lake stretched away and away into the distance. This expanse of water was an inconceivable pleasure to me, an incomparable splendour. At that time the idea became fixed in my mind that I must live near a lake; without water, I thought, nobody could live at all." The pleasure we derive from showers, saunas, swimming pools, ocean views and swimming in the sea testifies to the deep affinity that we feel for water — perhaps an echo of our amniotic state in our mother's womb, and possibly related also to the image of the unconscious itself as an unfathomable ocean.

Such thoughts point to the special value of water in relaxation — directly, through the senses, or in visualization exercises like the one opposite. It is also worth considering the other elements in this way. Air might seem at first to have more limited potential, but there is plenty of scope for visualizations on the themes of flying and clouds; and winds, or breezes, could be used as the basis of various enjoyable exercises for the senses.

Sea Tumbling

Exercise 22

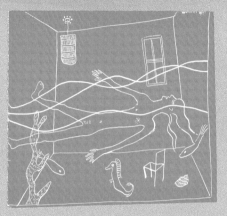

This relaxation exercise, by which you immerse yourself in the vastness of an imaginary sea and let its power cleanse you of anxiety, is a good choice for those who find detailed visualizations difficult: all that is needed is to conjure the swelling rhythms of the sea, and its turbulent energy. In the words of a well-known Tibetan Buddhist relaxation text, the aim is "to swim within the energies of the senses".

1 Lie comfortably in a quiet room. Hold up your arms, shake them and allow them to flop loosely at your sides. Close your eyes. Imagine lying at the sea's edge on an empty beach.

2 The tide is coming in. Gentle waves lap your feet and ankles and slowly — very slowly — move up your body until you are bathed in shallow water. As the water rises still further, sense yourself starting to float and being drawn by rhythmic currents out to sea.

3 Feel the big, undulating waves beginning to surge beneath you. Glide over their peaks and troughs.

4 Physically, turn on to your front. Now imaginatively ride the crest of a wave and, when it breaks, tumble over and over in its bright tunnel.

5 Be swept back up on to the shore, over smooth, warm sand. Do not move. Enjoy profound calm after your spell of freedom and exhilaration.

143

Green Balm

*T*he natural world transmits tranquillity. By contemplating the infinite variety of contours, colours, textures, scents and sounds, we can regain a sense of "oneness" with nature. Resting our eyes on a distant horizon, we relax the tight focus that the pressures of life often impose upon us. Next time you gaze at the skyline, visualize the muscles of the eyes losing all their tension, and think of how much good this is doing you. As figures in the landscape, we see ourselves within a broader perspective, and this offers a valuable corrective to self-preoccupation. In the Romantic Age, the sense of belittlement in the face of nature was so keenly felt that it was almost terrifying, and today we still tend to feel awed by a dramatic waterfall or towering cliff. Even in gentler landscapes we see ourselves differently, and some of our problems may come to seem less troublesome, or even completely illusory. The magic works gradually: the more time we spend in a natural landscape, the more our anxieties recede.

The efficacy of nature's balm is partly to do with shades of green, a hue psychologically linked with restfulness. If you have a small backyard, try filling it with different foliage shades and textures. Florists, of course, are convenient sources of supply, but you might prefer to make a habit of bringing cuttings, or perhaps still-life collections of seed-heads or fruits, indoors from the garden. You might consider letting one corner of the garden grow wild, as a haven for birds and insects.

Get to know the species names of your plants or flowers as a way to acknowledge their individual character. Learn the Latin as well as the common names. Speak the strange syllables aloud to yourself, and think of them lying like seeds in the garden of the mind.

Garden Meditations

Exercise 23

In cultures all over the world, plants and trees have been honoured for their spiritual associations. Next time you gaze at a tree, think of it as the Tree of Life, with its roots in the Underworld and an eagle high in its branches. Try to identify the qualities that made trees so special to the ancients. As a first step to acquainting yourself with your local trees, make a careful study of their leaves.

1 Pick a handful of different leaves from the trees or shrubs in your garden, or in a park nearby.

2 Sit comfortably and really study them – their shapes, colours and textures. Press them into your palms to feel their coolness. Trace each vein in each leaf with your finger. Meditate on the patterns you see.

3 Close your eyes, feel and smell the leaves. Try to remember which is which by touch and smell alone.

4 Become completely absorbed in the leaves, allowing worries, anxieties and negative thoughts to recede from consciousness.

5 As an extension to this exercise, refer to a book on plants or botany and learn the different names for the shapes of the leaves: palmate, pinnate, lanceolate, and so on.

6 Later, try adapting this exercise using flowers, stones or seashells as the objects of study.

Letting Go of the Past

*A*n adult fear of bees might originate in a childhood experience of being stung; or in our parents quickly whipping us out of the path of a bee with the words: "Be careful, this will hurt you." More often, the influence of the past on our personality, hopes and fears is complex, and difficult to trace. The past is by definition the repository of memories, and is also the journey on which we have picked up our life-skills: accordingly, we tend to believe that it will sustain and protect us. There are certainly great benefits in learning from our mistakes. But excessive attachment to the past can threaten present fulfilment.

Many of us are preoccupied with avoiding past disaster, even to the extent that we forget how to enjoy the present or how to hope for the future. If we have been badly hurt by someone, we may allow this to damage our self-esteem. We become anxious that the heartache will recur, and project this negativity into our current relationship, where it is reflected back at us. The relationship fails, which compounds our belief in the past, and heightens negative feelings about the future.

It is healthy to see past experiences as the spiritual wealth of our lives, our unfolding personal heritage. However, too great an attachment to these experiences can turn us in upon ourselves. The future then becomes blank, and frightening, and we fail to see how this emptiness can compare with the cluttered museum of memory. Afraid to leave our edifice, we see through a window the present pass by. Try to picture the museum of experience as a building in a landscape of extreme beauty. It is easy to walk away from the museum and become entranced by the unfamiliar terrain beyond. The museum is still there, over the horizon; but you have more exciting places to discover.

The Memory Album

Exercise 24

*We should never aim to repress our memories altogether, but neither should we try to live in them.
The following exercise is designed to close the book of the past in a spirit of new endeavour. We
may still refer back, but the most important thing is to concentrate on the future — to recognize
the potential for change and fill a brand-new album with experiences of a different flavour.*

1 Sit comfortably and close your eyes.
Conjure up some of the images from
the past that you tend to dwell on.
These might be faces, episodes or
places. Choose about ten memories,
more if you wish. A single image
might represent a phase of your life.

2 Imagine yourself pasting each of
these images into an album. Place
good memories alongside bad. Run
your eyes over this gallery of the past
and tell yourself that it will be a long
time before you deliberately re-visit

the archive of memory — although
some of the images might occur to
you fleetingly and spontaneously.

3 Imagine closing the album and
placing it on a high shelf in the least
visited room of your home.

4 Visualize a new, empty album,
which you look forward to filling. But
there is no need to think about pasting
in new images yet: you can do this
much later, after you have acquired a
wealth of new experiences.

147

Positive Recall

*O*nce we have accepted that the past is no place to live (see pp.146–7), it is helpful to see how experience can work as a learning resource, which if properly used can bring us closer to relaxation.

A memory episode typically contains problems, reactions, resolutions, ramifications. Such stories can never be re-lived – one cannot bathe in the same river twice, as an ancient Greek writer puts it. However, the episodes amount to a library of reference, a vast, multi-layered filing cabinet in the mind. Positive recall is a focused approach to memory that avoids the negative effects of making the past a place in which to lounge idly. At any time we can open a cabinet drawer and take out a file to use in the present for comparison and guidance – or simply to enjoy a few minutes of contented stock-taking. The important thing is that we are good housekeepers, and never leave the drawer open too long: we do not want the past spilling out and permanently cluttering up the present.

A single example will stand in for a host of possible situations. Imagine that you have to make a scintillating speech at work to wish an esteemed colleague farewell. As you read the jokes jotted down in your first draft, you may find it impossible to imagine their being met by anything other than embarrassed silence. However, if you open up the memory file containing the last time you made a speech at the office, you recall the laughter that greeted your witticisms. People have said that you have the comic gift. The speech may not be quite right yet: but work at it, in a spirit of self-belief, and you will effect your accustomed magic. The past, a gallery of your own potential, has shown you this. What you have done before, you can do again.

Pure Potential

Exercise 25

We can all draw energy from the past, by recollecting former achievements. Yet many people believe that they have lost touch with that younger, perhaps more vigorous self. This visualization exercise is designed to demonstrate that whatever it was that fuelled our triumphs in the past still exists as a living essence upon which we can draw again and again in our current endeavours.

1 Close your eyes and think about the situation that is troubling you. Remember times in the past when you overcame similar predicaments.

2 The problem, you tell yourself, is that you no longer have such reserves of strength or skill. The past is past, an abstract record, stored in the filing cabinet of memory.

3 Now think of a specific occasion in the past when you fulfilled your potential. Think of this occasion lying forgotten in a dusty file in the cabinet of the mind.

3 Walk, in your imagination, to the cabinet, and open the relevant drawer. You are amazed to see not files, but jars. You take out the jar that contains the memory in question and screw open the lid.

4 A strong perfume – essence of potential – emanates from the jar. You inhale it. As you do so, you take strength from the past.

Life, Death and Miracles

*T*he Irish literary genius Samuel Beckett wrote of a day that we all face, just like any other day, "only shorter". Mortality, we might think, is a most fearful notion. From the pharaohs of Egypt to the suicide cybercults of modern times, humankind has proffered countless explanations of exactly what happens to us once we die. Out of fear comes ingenuity.

Those with clearly defined religious beliefs would not thank a book like this for telling them how to come to terms with human perishability. In Western religion, good souls are reborn into heaven and bad souls into hell; in the East all souls are reborn but the status of the new birth depends on the moral standards attained in the previous life. The common theme here is that body and soul are separate. As the vehicle of the soul, the flesh of the body dies, while the soul, in whatever form, lives on. We do not need to believe in reincarnation, however, to understand the metaphor given to us by all these cultures: quality of life is determined not by external appearance or youthfulness but by the way we live, in thought, word and deed.

The key to a fulfilled life, without fear of death, is to fully appreciate that we are spiritual beings having a physical experience, rather than physical beings having a spiritual experience.

Proverbial wisdom

Even after our bodies have become dust, our words and actions will live on, in our children and grandchildren, in the memories of our family and friends, in the methods of our colleagues. So far-reaching is the network of cause and effect that our influence is incalculable. A pauper once persuaded a fabulously wealthy (but gullible) sultan to double his single piastre for each of the sultan's forty wives: the sum he accumulated in this way was more than a trillion piastres. Our spiritual legacy, the positive influence that we leave behind if only we concentrate on living good lives, is similarly out of all proportion to the initial stake.

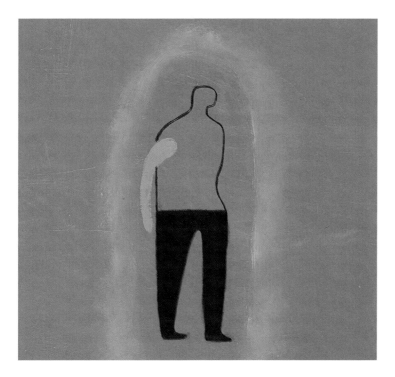

When we are afraid of something, we give it life in our mind. An abstraction takes on flesh, like a dragon bursting from the pages of a storybook into the real world. It then begins to affect us physically, making us tense and tired. So, paradoxically, the less fearful we are, the less we *have* to fear. A love of life and the will to live are a good basis for contentment during the time we have on earth.

Illness, especially if incurable, makes great demands upon our courage. It is hard to treat each day as a precious gift if each day is filled with pain. Yet we have all witnessed in others a way of dealing with illness that one can only call "grace" — the survival of the spirit's resources of fortitude, wisdom, generosity and humour into life's last painful phase. We can only hope, if such a fate befalls us, that grace will be in attendance.

Toward a Calm Future

An Eastern myth tells how a group of gods had a meeting to decide where to hide the "truth of the universe" from humanity. The first god suggests concealing it under the ocean, but the others shout him down, saying that people will build an underwater boat to take them there. A second god suggests hiding it the heavens, on a planet far from earth; but the other gods realize that a craft might be built to reach this destination also. Finally, a third god suggests that they hang the truth around the neck of every human being. The other gods agree that people will never look in this most obvious place for truth. And so they all do exactly as the third god has suggested.

When we look to the world to restore our peace of mind, or repair our lost hopes, or tell us how to live, we may never find the truth we seek, because that truth is buried deep inside us. Yet this is also the aspect of ourselves that we project to others: we are what we give. The idea that all our solutions lie within ourselves is wise and profound, but should never be taken to mean that there are two selves, outer and inner, and that so long as the inner self is strong, or daring, or eloquent, or loyal, or sensitive, then the outer self may be left to its own, purely functional devices — earning a living, washing the car, doing the dishes. The reality is that true forms of relaxation will not stop at the inner, private you, but will radiate out into the world beyond, transforming the outer, public you, and in time transforming others.

We cannot determine exactly what will happen tomorrow, or the next day, or in several years time, but we can set in motion positive energy that we hope will eventually come back to us. The ripples created when someone drops a stone into the middle of a pool of water radiate out until they hit the pool's

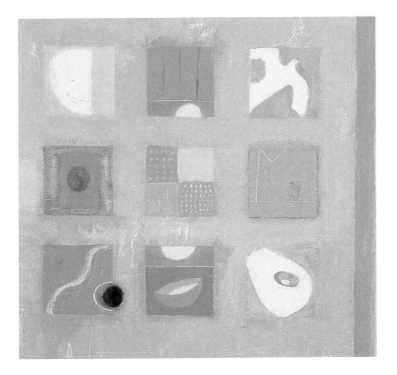

edges; whereupon they begin flowing back, in their complex cross-currents, toward the centre. In the same way, the blessings that we send out into the world will return to us. As we sow, so we shall reap: the principle of karma. We project our strong and confident virtue into the unknown, like a prayer winging its way to the divinity; and the prayer is rewarded in time with revelations.

We must face ourselves, understand who we are, find value in ourselves, and act according to that value. If we follow this self-awareness route toward contentment, instead of running away toward escapist sources of relaxation, then our positive energy will transmit itself out into the future. And every time we arrive at the future, we shall find that it was waiting for us all along — primed to receive us by all that we had thought, said and done in the past.

Bibliography

Benson, Herbert
The Relaxation Response
William Morrow (New York)
Gawain, Shakti
Creative Visualization
Bantam (London and New York)
Goleman, Daniel
Emotional Intelligence: Why it can
Matter More than IQ
Bloomsbury (London)
Hudson, John
Instant Meditation for Everyone
Lorenz Books (London)
Jarmey, Chris
Principles of Shiatsu
Thorsons (London and San Francisco)
Jeffers, Dr Susan
Feel the Fear and Do it Anyway
End the Struggle and Dance with Life
both books published by Coronet
(London)
Kennerley, Dr Helen
Overcoming Anxiety: A self-help guide using
Cognitive Behavioural Techniques
Robinson (London)
Lao Zi (trans. D. C. Lau)
Dao de Jing
Penguin Classics (London and
New York)
Lindenfield, G.
Assert Yourself
Thorsons (London and San Francisco)
Madders, Jane
Stress and Relaxation: Self-help
Techniques for Everyone
Optima (London)

Maxwell-Hudson, Clare
The Complete Book of Massage
Dorling Kindersley (London
and New York)
Mills, J. W.
Coping with Stress
Wiley (Sussex, England)
Mitchell, Stewart
Massage: A Practical Introduction
Element (Dorset, England and
Rockport, Massachussetts)
Patel, Dr Chandra
The Complete Guide to Stress
Management
Vermilion/Ebury Press (London)
Reps, Paul
Zen Flesh, Zen Bones
Arkana/Penguin (London
and New York)
Tresidder, Megan
The Secret Language of Love
Chronicle Books (San Francisco)
Watts, Murray and Professor
Cary L. Cooper
Relax: Dealing with Stress
BBC Books (London)
Wilson, Paul
Instant Calm
The Little Book of Calm
both books published by
Penguin (London and
New York)
Wildwood, Chrissie
The Complete Guide to Reducing
Stress
Piatkus (London)

Index

Acknowledgments

*The publishers should like to thank
the following magazines for their kind
permission to reproduce artworks
by Sarah Ball:*
pp.81, 99, 105 and 135
    The New Scientist
p.45 *Woman and Home Magazine*

The background images on
pp.7, 17, 19, 25, 29, 39, 49,
51, 53, 59, 61, 65, 69, 71,
93, 103, 119, 127, 137, 139,
141, 143, 145, 147, 149 are
details of Sarah Ball's work.

*For further information on any of the
ideas or exercises in this book, you can
contact Mike George in London by
fax 0181 451 6480; or by e-mail
mike@bkwsugch.demon.co.uk.*